one thousand gifts

DEVOTIONAL

Also by Ann Voskamp

One Thousand Gifts

Selections from One Thousand Gifts

one thousand gifts

DEVOTIONAL

REFLECTIONS ON FINDING EVERYDAY GRACES

ANN VOSKAMP

ZONDERVAN®

ZONDERVAN

One Thousand Gifts Devotional
Copyright © 2012 by Ann Morton Voskamp

This title is also available as a Zondervan ebook. Visit www.zondervan.com/ebooks.

This title is also available in a Zondervan audio edition. Visit www.zondervan.fm.

Requests for information should be addressed to:

Zondervan, 3900 Sparks Dr SE, *Grand Rapids, Michigan 49546*

Library of Congress Cataloging-in-Publication Data

Voskamp, Ann, 1973–
    One thousand gifts devotional : reflections on finding everyday graces / Ann Voskamp.
      p. cm
    ISBN 978-0-310-31544-5 (hardcover)
    1. Christian life—Meditations. 2. Devotional literature. I. Title.
  BV4832.3.V68   2012
  242—dc23   2012031077

All Scripture quotations, unless otherwise indicated, are taken from The Holy Bible, *New International Version®, NIV®.* Copyright © 1973, 1978, 1984, 2011 by Biblica, Inc.® Used by permission. All rights reserved worldwide. Quotations marked KJV are taken from the King James Version of the Bible. Quotations marked NASB are taken from the New American Standard Version® NASB®. Copyright © 1960, 1962, 1963, 1968, 1971, 1972, 1973, 1975, 1977, 1995 by The Lockman Foundation. Used by permission (www.Lockman.org). Quotations marked AMP are taken from The Amplified Bible. Copyright © 1954, 1958, 1962, 1964, 1965, 1987 by The Lockman Foundation. All rights reserved. Used by permission (www.Lockman.org). Quotations marked MSG are taken from The Message. Copyright © 1993, 1994, 1995, 1996, 2000, 2001, 2002 by Eugene H. Peterson. Used by permission of NavPress Publishing Group. Quotations marked ESV are taken from the English Standard Version. Copyright © 2001 by Crossway Bibles, a division of Good News Publishers. All rights reserved. Used by permission. Quotations marked BBE are taken from the Bible in Basic English. Quotations marked NEB are taken from The New English Bible. Copyright © Oxford University Press and Cambridge University Press 1961, 1970. Quotations marked NCV are taken from the New Century Version. Copyright © 2005 by Thomas Nelson, Inc. All rights reserved. Used by permission.

Any Internet addresses (websites, blogs, etc.) and telephone numbers in this book are offered as a resource. They are not intended in any way to be or imply an endorsement by Zondervan, nor does Zondervan vouch for the content of these sites and numbers for the life of this book.

Published in association with William K. Jensen Literary Agency, 119 Bampton Court, Eugene, Oregon 97404.

Cover design: Michelle Lenger
Cover photography: Ann Voskamp with Hope Voskamp
Cover background: iStockphoto®
Interior design: Beth Shagene

Printed in the United States of America

To the Oregonian Three

who have always believed that standing straight into wind
is how to fly on His wings of grace

contents

your journey by grace

It all began quite spontaneously, unintentionally. One of those things God grows up in the most unexpected places.

A friend dared me to start counting one thousand things I loved. I took the dare, accepted the challenge, kept track of one thousand things, one thousand gifts—a thousand *graces*—on a quiet, unassuming blog. Before I knew it, thankfulness to God began to fully change me.

What I actually found—startling!—was more daily wonder and surprising beauty than I ever expected. And in a few short years, this daily hunt for God's grace, His glory, *had* ushered me into a fuller life. A life of joy! Over the past several years, I've listed over four thousand gifts ... and I continue. Once one has begun, has tasted and known He is God, who can stop giving Him glory? Thousands more have begun their own lists—in jail cells and by death beds, in third-world slums and by faith alone—and it's not overstatement to say that giving Him thanks has made me—and innumerable others—overcomers.

How did all this happen?

A few years ago, I decided to try to live this giving thanks as I believe Jesus did each day, regardless of His circumstances. And what I found was that in giving thanks for each moment and savoring it as bread from His hand, I'd find sustenance and the grace of God Himself in it. I wrote a book about this gratitude journey called *One Thousand Gifts*. I didn't start with any specific steps, but through this intentional, daily practice of giving thanks, I found myself on a transformative journey that affected every aspect of my life—including all the broken places. God began to show me the graces, the love gifts, that were right before me, waiting to be noticed, waiting to be received. This easily overlooked stuff, the small—and especially the hard—became for me a life-giving stream of *joy in Him.*

Even when I am sometimes impatient or unwilling, when I face conflict and heartache, I've begun to accept that even the impossible is a possible opportunity to thank God, to experience the goodness and grace of the Giver of all!

There is always only more grace.

And it's always more than I expect.

And you? You in the midst, you in the mire, are you too thinking about counting one thousand gifts, about making your life all about joy in Christ, about loving God and enjoying Him forever? There is so much joy in seeing how He uses our simple act of *noticing* the blessings He bestows all around us to transform our lives and the lives of those we touch.

So here is how I suggest you begin this journey by grace, begin your own gift list, count all the ways He loves you:

Pray. Start with a simple request, making it the refrain of your day: "God, open the eyes of my heart." This journey must be Spirit-led, every day.

Receive. Open your hand to the simple, daily gifts, writing down all the unique and ordinary things you notice, from the grand and obvious to the humble and hidden.

Praise. Praise Him for the unexpected and the unlikely, for the daily and the difficult, and the graces in disguise. The more you count, the more gifts you will see. Do not disdain the small. The moments add up, and we might come to believe it—*the whole earth is full of His glory!*

Beyond that, there is no method or formula. There is simply a willingness to bend to receive, to begin to take note of the daily love God unfurls.

What could be simpler, more glorious, than doing what we were made for?

It could be like this: I found setting a goal of one thousand gifts over a few months beneficial—it kept me attending to all the ways He whispers, "I love you." Some folks count ten graces a day, others just three a day to total one thousand in a year, while still others spend one day a week intensely, wildly counting, a jarring wide-awake. Whatever you do, the practice is intended to be a way of cultivating a habit, of learning to live praise, to make gratitude and joy your default, to move thanksgiving away from a holiday to a *lifestyle*—that all the days might be holy and set apart for real joy.

These sixty reflections chronicle my discovery, each one like a singular tree in a lush forest of graces. While every journey is unique, my humble prayer is that sharing these glimpses will companion and encourage you in your own prayerful discovery of a lifestyle of Christ-focus and communion. Of how extravagantly God loves you and how desperately you need Him every moment. Most of all, I hope these entries expand your view of the endless and matchless grace of an overflowing God. Just turn to the back of this book, press open that journaling space, and begin your own list of one thousand gifts— *take the dare to fully live!*

Oh, let the gift hunt begin! God is waiting to reveal so much through your desire to know Him more deeply and completely—but His grace is only experienced *directly*. The most important thing is simply to begin.

May God bless your journey with the greatest gift of all—more and more of Himself!

All is grace.

Ann

surprising grace

This is what the LORD says:

"In the time of my favor I will answer you,
    and in the day of salvation I will help you;
I will keep you and will make you
    to be a covenant for the people,
to restore the land
    and to reassign its desolate inheritances."

Isaiah 49:8

That field of beans west of the barn, it looked gaunt come October, bean pods all hanging like bony ribs.

Whenever the wind sighed, the whole field just rattled skinny.

That's how my dad always spoke of a railish man, that you could count his ribs. Nothing in me wanted to count those beans, know the yield, from that spare field.

When my husband, the Farmer, rolled the combine in and lowered the combined head to bring those beans in, I sat beside him, raised my voice to ask it above the combine's working engine: "Is it possible that something that doesn't look like anything—can still amount to something?"

The field, it was hard to even look at it. I've known a face in a mirror much like that.

"Well—it isn't much to look at, is it?" The Farmer looks up from the combine's steering wheel, looks across the field to the north. "Weedy. And thin."

The white of the sow thistle seeds mingles with the dust. This field had no rain in July, and a man can't make a sky give. He can just make the knees bend and the hands raise. The harvest looked like a failure. I've known this, been this, am this.

The first time thanksgiving is ever mentioned in Scripture, this is what we read:

> And this is the law of the sacrifice of peace offerings that one may offer to the LORD. If he offers it for a thanksgiving, then he shall offer with the thanksgiving sacrifice unleavened loaves mixed with oil, unleavened wafers smeared with oil, and loaves of fine flour well mixed with oil. With the sacrifice of his peace offerings for thanksgiving he shall bring his offering with loaves of leavened bread.
>
> *Leviticus 7:11–13 ESV*

The first time thanksgiving is mentioned in Scripture, the thanksgiving offering was part of the peace offering. Could that be the thing?

Could it be—no one receives the peace of God without giving thanks to God? Is thankfulness really but the deep, contented breath of peacefulness? Is this why God asks us to give thanks even when things look a failure? When there doesn't seem much to give thanks for?

The beans rattle through the combine, the auger filling the bin with golden beans like bread rising slow.

There were to be ten offerings of bread in every thank offering of the Israelites.

The first were like crackers. The second like wafers. These were known for their thinness. This was the order of thanks.

The thanks began for the thin things, the wafer things that almost weren't, and the way the people of God give thanks is first to give thanks for even the meager and unlikely.

Then it came, thanks for the leavened bread. Why would leaven, yeast—that which is seen in Scripture as impure, unwanted—why would leaven be included as part of the thanks offering?

Authentic thanks is always for *all* things, because our God is a God kneading *all* things into a bread that sustains. Paul gave "glory in tribulations" (Romans 5:3 KJV) and took "pleasure in infirmities, in reproaches, in necessities, in persecutions, in distresses for Christ's sake" (2 Corinthians 12:10 KJV), and he knew that which didn't look like anything good might yield good, all in the hand of a good God.

To bring the sacrifice of thanksgiving means to sacrifice our understanding of what is beneficial and thank God for everything because He is benevolent. A sacrifice of thanks lays down our perspective and raises hands in praise anyways—*always*. A sacrifice is, by definition, not an easy thing—but it is a sacred thing.

There is this: We give thanks to God not because of how we feel but because of who He is.

"See it on the monitor?" The Farmer points to the screen to the right of the combine's steering wheel. "See the numbers, how many bushels an acre? If you didn't see the numbers, you'd never guess it, would you? It's yielding higher than it looks." He's shaking his head in happy wonder.

"Really? How can that be?" The numbers on the screen defy the seemingly sparse and stunted crop, and I'm laughing incredulous.

"I know! I know ..." The Farmer smiles, glances down at the beans feeding into the combine head, one eye still watching number of bushels on the screen.

He who is grateful for little is given much laughter ... and it's counting the ways He loves, *this* is what multiplies joy.

The life that counts blessings discovers its yielding more than it seems.

Why don't I keep more of an eye on the number of His graces? Why don't I want to know that even though it doesn't seem like there's been enough rain, He reigns and He is enough and the bounty is greater than it appears?

The thin places might be the places closest to God and the skinny places might be fuller than they seem, and who isn't full when they have Christ?

"Look how many seeds were really hiding in this pod!"

Little Shalom, she calls to me walking back across the field. "Count them, Mama."

"Yes," I say. "Yes, let's count."

And there's this counting the ribs of the field, graces filling unexpectedly, thanksgiving always this walking toward peace, and I see it.

See it—how the Farmer waves to me from the harvest seat, his hand turned willingly up to the sky.

God, cause me to know it afresh today: the life that counts blessings discovers its yielding much more than it seems. And my life yields most when I yield most to You.

choosing grace

His secret purpose framed from the very beginning
[is] to bring us to our full glory.

1 Corinthians 2:7 NEB

They lay her gravestone flat into the earth, a black granite slab engraved with no dates, only the five letters of her name. Aimee. It means "loved one." How she was. We had loved her. And with the laying of my sister's gravestone, the closing up of her deathbed, so closed our lives.

Closed to any notion of grace.

Really, when you bury a child—or when you just simply get up every day and live life raw—you murmur the question soundlessly. No one hears. *Can there be a good God?* How can He be good when babies die, and marriages implode, and dreams blow away, dust in the wind? Where is grace bestowed when cancer gnaws and loneliness aches and nameless places in us soundlessly die, break off without reason, erode away? Where hides this joy of the Lord, this God who fills the earth with good things, and how do I fully live when life is full of hurt? How do I wake up to joy and grace and beauty and all that is the fullest life when I must stay numb to losses and crushed dreams and all that empties me out?

Is this the toxic air of the world, this atmosphere we inhale, burning into our lungs, this *No, God? No, God, we won't take what You give. No, God, Your plans are a gutted, bleeding mess, and I didn't sign up for this and You really thought I'd go for this? No, God, this is ugly and this is a mess and can't You get anything right and just haul all this pain out of here and I'll take it from here, thanks. And God? Thanks for nothing.* Isn't this the human inheritance, the legacy of the Garden?

Everywhere, a world pocked with scarcity.

I hunger for filling in a world that is starved.

But from that Garden beginning, God has had a different purpose for us. His intent, since He bent low and breathed His life into the dust of our lungs, since He kissed us into being, has never been to slyly orchestrate our ruin. And yet, I have found it: He does have surprising, secret purposes.

I open a Bible, and His plans, startling, lie there barefaced. It's hard to believe it, when I read it, and I have to come back to it many times, feel long across those words, make sure they are real. His love letter forever silences any doubts. He means to rename us—to return us to our true names, our truest selves.

He means to heal our soul holes.

From the very beginning, that Eden beginning, that has always been and always is, to this day, His secret purpose—our return to *our full glory. Appalling*—that He would! Us, unworthy. And yet since we took a bite out of the fruit and tore into our own souls, that drain hole where joy seeps away, God's had this wild secretive plan. *He means to fill us with glory again.* With glory and grace.

Grace, it means "favor," from the Latin *gratia*. It connotes a free readiness. A free and ready favor. That's grace. It is one thing to choose to take the grace offered at the cross. But to choose to live as one *filling* with His grace? Choosing to *fill* with *all* that He freely gives and fully live—with glory and grace and God?

I know it but I don't want to: it is a choice.

Living with losses, I may choose to still say yes.
Choose to say yes to what He freely gives.

~

*God of all gifts, thank You. Thank You! For the grace to choose to see.
I choose to say yes today to all You give. Do the work in me—I want to
more fully live.*

first grace

But the basic reality of God is plain enough.
Open your eyes and there it is!
By taking a long and thoughtful look at what God has created,
people have always been able to see
what their eyes as such can't see: . . .
the mystery of his divine being.

Romans 1:19 – 20 MSG

It's after I cut the squash right open.

The two halves split and quartered there on the cutting board.

After the paintbrushes are washed out, after the pawns of the chess game are all returned to their squares, after the potatoes are baked and served, the dinner plates are pushed back empty. The Farmer splits the Word right open then and that's when I'm cut to the quick.

"First, I thank my God . . ." That's what it reads, right there in Romans 1. The Farmer reads it slow — what should always come first in everything. And Paul writes more, peels back the hot holiness of God. I hold it there in my hands. The holy words that hollow me out.

The wrath of God is being revealed from heaven against all the
godlessness and wickedness of people, who suppress the truth by
their wickedness, since what may be known about God is plain to

them, because God has made it plain to them. For since the creation of the world God's invisible qualities — his eternal power and divine nature — have been clearly seen, being understood from what has been made, so that people are without excuse.

For although they knew God, they neither glorified him as God nor gave thanks to him ... as they did not think it worthwhile to retain the knowledge of God, so God gave them over to a depraved mind, so that they do what ought not to be done.

Romans 1:18 – 21, 28

The light fills the drinking cups still on the table. I can feel its warmth on the nape of my neck. Spring coming. The heat of it melting everything cold.

One of the best writers I've read and a kind friend, pastor, and fellow Canadian, Mark Buchanan, asked the most critical questions of them all: "What initially sparks God's anger? What is the root sin, the molten core of wickedness and godlessness — that convinces God to turn us over?"[1]

Isn't that what we have to figure out? It's right there in Romans 1. It's not the sinfulness you'd think it'd be: It's the thanklessness — that we do. It's our thanklessness that first stirs the full wrath of God.

The beginnings of Genesis and Romans 1 pivot on the same point: Eve's thanklessness for all God does give and her resentfulness of the one fruit He doesn't give, this is the catalyst of the fall. Which Romans 1 confirms: "For although they knew God, they neither glorified him as God nor *gave thanks* to him, but their thinking became futile, and their foolish hearts were darkened."

Our fall is always first a failure to give thanks.

The pride of thanklessness always comes before the fall. God makes Himself plain and there's no excuse — but they did not give Him thanks.

I have done this and just this morning, there spooning potatoes. The house upended with ridiculously messy and wondrous living. Paint smeared on a shirt, across a table. The chess loser in loud tears. The stringy innards of squash all over the counter. Instead of falling on my knees in thanks, I fall into sin and anger.

When I refuse to give God thanks? God lets our very lives become refuse.

I'd do well to stitch it into the fabric of me: *A lack of doxology leads to depravity.*

That is what Buchanan discovers in Scripture, right there in Romans: "The heart of wickedness and godlessness is that: a refusal to glorify God. It's the refusal to thank Him."[2]

Wickedness isn't rooted primarily in some ghetto, on some shady backstreet. No, as Buchanan states, "All the wickedness in the world begins with an act of forgetting."[3]

I nod slow.

In a thousand infinite ways God turns His glory around for us to see, but we can shrug; we can turn a blind eye. And so He lets it come, what we want—and everything, us, it all goes black.

There is light at the table, these open pages filling with it.

Isn't that what Paul is saying? When, in light of everything, we don't turn to God in thanks, God gives in to what we want—and turns us over to the dark ...

Turn in thanks and everything turns—and God doesn't turn away.

And there is this: If all the dismembering wickedness in the world begins with an act of forgetting—then the act of literally counting blessings literally re-members us to God. This is the making whole.

After lunch, I clean off the counter, gather up the halved squash and their inners, and afterward turn to the journal and jot down another note of thanks, for the time and the light to see by.

For all these halves, they are finding their wholes.

Father God, You are the Begetter of grace. Forgive me for being a forgetter of thanks. This is no trivial thing. It leads to wicked things. Hear the cry of my heart: Forgive me for not giving You thanks. If thanks is the highest form of thought—make it my first thought. Turn me toward thanks first —so my life doesn't turn into the last thing I'd hoped for. Turn me toward You first—first things first means to give You thanks first.

thinking grace

Through Jesus, therefore,
let us continually offer to God a sacrifice of praise—
the fruit of lips that openly profess his name.

Hebrews 13:15

When the rope pulls tight, Levi holds on—and it looks like happy wonder might right split him.

The kid, he's all snow-caked—all celebration.

He's making me grin. Life could be like that—giving way to the celebration of fully living.

He's making me the child—the laughter falling like snow and his cheeks all red, winter and wonder right in him, and his father winks at me and I lay on the snow and this moment right here, it warms right through.

Who can't laugh with him, this sledding straight to the sheer edge?

He does go down more than once or twice.

I wait for tears.

And I'm the fool not knowing what it's all about. It's there in his eyes: the thrill is in the trying what doesn't seem possible.

Isn't that always the place where fear meets faith and the face of God?

The snow's bluing in twilight. The dog's panting happy. The boy's all full of life, wonder-filled.

The sun is doing its own sliding down. I try to memorize all this wonderful—the faith and the falls and the fully living.

Robert Frost is right: "An hour of winter day might seem too short."[4] And there are Eden days—days you want the boy to stay freckled and laughing loud and the light to linger longer and the dog to keep running you young.

It's not trite, this waking to wonder, giving thanks for all this.

Thanks isn't shallow Pollyanna-ism. Didn't Chesterton suggest that?

"I would maintain that thanks are the highest form of thought, and that gratitude is happiness doubled by wonder."[5]

And I wonder if this is why thanks is the highest form of thought—because this is always the right order of things: Us laid low. Before God on High.

Isn't this what's partly awry in the world? The world needs fewer complaints and more thanks—those engaged in the highest thoughts.

The world needs more men and women living thanks, thinking loftiest.

Why would we ever tire of bending low in thanking—*thanking*—this highest form of thinking?

This is what all the great artists and thinkers do—they stay awake to the wonder of God's world. Great thinkers are the grateful thankers —the real greats live gratefully.

And is this the art of life—to keep awake to the wonders in His Word and this world?

Isn't it wonder that sparks love?

Levi swings round on his sled, chasing joy, that thing that swings open everything.

He yells at me as he flies by. "Isn't this great?"

And I smile thanks for the wonder of here. Thanks, that thing that makes you the child full of wonder, the great thinker, the kingdom of heaven belonging to those who are like the children.

And the trees at sunset, they're lit aflame right down there in the woods.

~⌒

Father God, make me never tire of the highest form of thinking— thanking. Make today great— by causing me to think gratefully. Engage me in the highest thoughts— gratefully laid low before You.

here-now grace

And he took bread, gave thanks and broke it,
and gave it to them . . .
Luke 22:19

I remember once sitting at the hairdresser's. The woman beside me reads, and I read her title in the reflection of the mirror: *1,000 Places to See Before You Die.* Is that it? Are there physical places I simply must see before I stop breathing within time, before I inhale eternity?

Why? To say that I've had reason to bow low? To say that I've seen beauty? To say that I've been arrested by wonder?

Isn't it here? Can't I find it *here?*

These very real lungs will breathe in more than 11,000 liters of air today, and tonight over our farm will rise the Great Hexagon of the blazing winter stars — Sirius, Rigel, ruby Aldebran, Capella, the fiery Gemini twins, the Procyon, and in the center, scarlet Betelgeuse, the red supergiant larger than twice the size of earth's orbit around the sun.

Isn't it here? The wonder? Why do I spend so much of my living hours struggling to see it? Do we truly stumble so blind that we must be affronted with *blinding* magnificence for our blurry soul-sight to recognize grandeur? The very same surging magnificence that cascades over our every day here. Who has time or eyes to notice?

I don't need more time to breathe so that I may experience more locales, possess more, accomplish more. Because wonder really could be here—for the seeing eyes.

The face of Jesus flashes. Jesus, the God-Man with his own termination date. Jesus, the God-Man who came to save me from prisons of fear and guilt and depression and sadness. With an expiration of less than twelve hours, what does Jesus count as all-important?

"And he took bread, *gave thanks* and broke it, and gave it to them" (Luke 22:19, emphasis added).

I read it slowly. In the original language, "he gave thanks" reads "*eucharisteo.*" I underline it on the page.

The root word of *eucharisteo* is *charis,* meaning "grace." Jesus took the bread and saw it as grace and gave thanks. He took the bread and knew it to be *gift* and gave thanks.

But there is more, and I read it. *Eucharisteo,* thanksgiving, envelopes the Greek word for grace, *charis.* But it also holds its derivative, the Greek word *chara,* meaning "joy." *Joy.* Ah ... yes. I might be needing me some of that. That might be what the quest for more is all about —that which Augustine claimed, "Without exception ... all try their hardest to reach the same goal, that is, joy."[6]

I breathe deep, like a sojourner finally coming home. This has always been the goal of the fullest life—joy. And my life knew exactly how elusive that slippery three-letter word, *joy,* can be. My whole being responded to that one word. I longed for more life, for more *holy joy.*

That's what I was struggling to reach, to seize. Joy. But where can I seize this holy grail of joy? I look back down to the page. Was this the clue to the quest of all most important? Deep *chara* joy is found only at the table of the *euCHARisteo*—the table of thanksgiving. I sit there long ... wondering ... is it that simple?

Is the height of my *chara* joy dependent on the depths of my *eucharisteo* thanks?

So then as long as thanks is possible—I think this through—as long as thanks is possible, then joy is always possible. *Joy is always possible.*

Whenever, meaning—"now"; *wherever*, meaning—"here."

The holy grail of joy is not in some exotic location or some emotional mountain peak experience. The joy wonder could be here! Here, in the messy, piercing ache of now, joy might be—unbelievably —possible! The only place we need see before we die is this place of seeing God, here and now.

I whisper it out loud, let the tongue feel these sounds, the ear hear their truth.

Charis. Grace.

Eucharisteo. Thanksgiving.

Chara. Joy.

A triplet of stars, a constellation in the black.

This search for the constellation in the dark—grace, thanksgiving, joy—it might be like that—a reaching for stars.

God, thank You for showing me the beauty in all these here-now wonders that You've placed before me—to do good and right work in me. Cause me to see all that encircles me today with new eyes of thankfulness.

anti-anxiety grace

Surely I have composed and quieted my soul;
Like a weaned child rests against his mother,
My soul is like a weaned child within me.
Psalm 131:2 NASB

There are birds at the feeders, chickadees. They flit, nervous. I watch the light in the trees, the way it falls across the walls. Across the calendar and to-do lists, and I try to remember to breathe.

John Calvin and I, we both remember the year we were four.

The year I was four, my sister was crushed under the wheels of a truck in our driveway. That is my first memory, the day Aimee was killed.

Fears have formed me.

John Calvin's mother died the year he was four. Scholar and historian William Bouwsma describes Calvin as "a singularly anxious man."[7] Calvin buried all three babies born to him and his wife. He said he found in the Psalms "all the griefs, sorrows, fears, doubts, hopes, cares, perplexities, in short all the distracting emotions with which the minds of men are wont to be agitated."[8] The man understood fear.

Clouds have skirted in heavy from the west. The walls in the kitchen have fallen gray and silent. Joshua's playing it quietly, up and down the piano this morning, the *Music Box Dancer.* A friend laid out in great detail this weekend how the economy is about to implode. Chronic illness flares. Teenagers ask big questions. I keep smoothing out calendar pages, pushing things back. *How do you remember how to dance?*

What is the answer to anxiety? Joshua's playing so sure, the house lilting, tilting with happiness. That's what Calvin wrote. "The stability of the world depends on this rejoicing of God in his works." And again, "If on earth, such praise of God does not come to pass, . . . then the whole order of nature will be thrown into confusion."[9]

Our worlds reel unless we rejoice. A song of thanks steadies everything.

The answer to anxiety is the adoration of Christ.

My Bible lays open beside my gratitude journal. There are piano lessons today and already a little brother's in tears, word-bruised by a big brother, and sisters are arguing loud over whose turn it is to make the bed, and I've snapped, exasperated, ugly, at a whining middle kid who doesn't want to stomp through snow and cold to get eggs from the henhouse. Anxiety can wear anger's mask. Fear of failing, of falling, of falling behind, it can make us fierce. Life can be messy before nine in the morning.

Joshua's tripping on notes. The thermometer out on the tree, its mercury is sluggish and heavy. Hard frost lines windows. How to breathe and dance?

"We are cold when it comes to rejoicing in God!" wrote Calvin. "Hence, we need to exercise ourselves in it and employ all our senses in it — our feet, our hands, our arms and all the rest — that they all might serve in the worship of God and so magnify Him."[10]

That's it. When exasperation mounts, *exercise* our song, employ all our senses.

I use my hand, pick up the pen, and write down a few more gifts — *employ* the senses to see and magnify God in that gratitude journal.

I warm. Joshua's practicing the chorus. Exercise. Employ. *Exalt.*

The answer to anxiety is always to *exalt Christ.*

The chickadees scuttle at the feeder and fly, warmth on the wing. I watch from the window. A child presses into me and the window and we have time. There is wonder. Everything absorbs into thanksgiving.

Calvin said that. "If we compare a hawk with the residue of the whole world, it is nothing. And yet if so small a portion of God's work ought to ravish us and amaze us, what ought all his works do when we come to the full numbering of them?"[11]

Ravish and amaze? Did Calvin number too? Come to the full numbering, the one thousand, the endless numbering of the infinite grace of God? My pen is on the counter.

Joshua's playing perfect joy now, the *Music Box Dancer*, finding all the right notes, exercising all this exaltation. And I'm thinking no one sees me in the kitchen spinning around, exercising feet and hands and arms and all the rest, smiling happiness anyways.

Dancing brave and unafraid anyways.

～

Holy Father, John Calvin said that the stability of the world depends on the rejoicing in Your works. Doesn't my world also stabilize when I rejoice in Your works? I'm echoing Calvin today: "What ought all Your works do when we come to the full numbering of them?" I too might dance. Cause me to remember it today, Lord: adore Christ to combat anxiety.

trusting grace

Do not be anxious about anything,
but in every situation,
by prayer and petition,
with thanksgiving,
present your requests to God.

Philippians 4:6

Anxiety has been my natural posture; stiffness, my default. The way I curl my toes up, tight retreat. How I angle my jaw, braced, chisel the brow with the lines of distrust. How I don't fold my hands in prayer, how I weld them into tight fists of control. *Always control—pseudopower from the pit.* How I refuse to relinquish worry, like a babe a mother won't forsake, an identity.

Do I hold worry close as this ruse of control, this pretense that I'm the one who will determine the course of events as I stir and churn and ruminate? Worry is the facade of taking action when prayer really is. And *stressed*, this pitched word that punctuates every conversation, is it really my attempt to prove how indispensable I am? Or is it more? Maybe disguising my deep fears as stress seems braver somehow.

An untroubled heart relaxes, trusts, leans assured into His ever-dependable arms. Trust, it's the antithesis of stress. "Oh, the joys of those who trust the LORD" (Psalm 40:4 NLT). But how to learn trust like that? Can trust be conjured up simply by sheer will, on command?

I can't fill with joy until I learn how to trust: "May the God of hope fill you with all *joy* and peace as you *trust* in him, so that you may overflow" (Romans 15:13, emphasis added). The full life, the one spilling joy and peace, happens only as I come to trust the caress of the Lover, Lover who never burdens His children with shame or self-condemnation but keeps stroking the fears with gentle grace.

If I believe, then I must let go and trust. Belief in God has to be more than mental assent, more than a clichéd exercise in cognition. What is saving belief if it isn't the radical dare to wholly trust?

Pisteuo is used more than two hundred times in the New Testament, most often translated as "belief." But it changes everything when I read that *pisteuo* ultimately means "to put one's faith in; to trust." *Belief is a verb, something that you do.*

Then the truth is that authentic, saving belief must be also? The very real, everyday *action* of trusting ... Then a true saving faith is a faith that gives thanks, a faith that sees God, a faith that deeply trusts? How would *eucharisteo* help me trust?

I read the verse several times in the Amplified Bible on an afternoon while young hands work scales up and down the piano keys. "Jesus replied, 'This is the work (service) that God asks of you: that you believe in the One Whom He has sent [that you cleave to, trust, rely on, and have faith in His Messenger]' " (John 6:29 AMP). That's my daily work, the work God asks of me? To trust.

Sometimes, too often, I don't want to muster the energy. Stress and anxiety seem easier. Easier to let a mind run wild with the worry than to exercise discipline, to rein her in, slip the blinders on, and train her to walk steady in certain assurance, not spooked by the specters looming ahead. Are stress and worry evidences of a soul too lazy, too undisciplined, to keep gaze fixed on God? To stay in love? I don't like to ask these questions, sweep out these corners where eyes glare from shadows.

Stress brings no joy. Isn't joy worth the effort of trust?

> "This is the work (service) that God asks of you: that you believe in the One Whom He has sent [that you cleave to, trust, rely on, and have faith in His Messenger]."

And I know and haltingly confess: Much of the worry in my own life has been a failure to believe ... a wariness to thank and trust the loving hand of God.

I make soup and I bake bread, and I know my supreme need is joy in God and I know I can't experience deep joy in God until I deep trust in God. I shine sinks and polish through to the realization that trusting God is my most urgent need.

> He who did not spare his own Son, but gave him up for us all—how will he not also, along with him, graciously give us all things?
>
> *Romans 8:32*

He gave us Jesus. *Jesus! Gave Him up for us all.* If we have only one memory, isn't this one enough? Why is this the memory I most often take for granted?

He cut open the flesh of the God-Man and let the blood. He washed our grime with the bloody grace. He drove the iron ore through His own vein. Doesn't that memory alone suffice? Need there be anything more? If God didn't withhold from us His very own Son, will God withhold *anything* we need?

If trust must be earned, hasn't God unequivocally earned our trust with the bark on the raw wounds, the thorns pressed into the brow, your name on the cracked lips? How will He not also graciously give us all things He deems best and right? He's already given the incomprehensible.

Christ our Crossbeam.

The counting of all blessings is ultimately summed up in One.

The radical wonder of it stuns me happy, hushes me still: *It's all Christ.* Every moment, every event, every happening.

It's all in Christ and in Christ we are always safe.

~

Lord, cause me to take a deep breath right now and really trust in my Savior—that He really saves. Thank You, Lord; in my Savior I am always safe.

urgent grace

As a father has compassion on his children,
    so the LORD has compassion on those who fear him;
for he knows how we are formed,
    he remembers that we are dust.

Psalm 103:13–14

God gives us time. But who has time for God? This may not make any good sense.

A well-known pastor was once asked what his most profound regret in life was: "Being in a hurry." That is what he said.

> Getting to the next thing without fully entering the thing in front of me. I cannot think of a single advantage I've ever gained from being in a hurry.
>
> But a thousand broken and missed things, tens of thousands, lie in the wake of all the rushing.... Through all that haste I thought I was *making up time*. It turns out I was *throwing it away*.[12]

In our rushing, bulls in china shops, we break our own lives. Haste makes waste. The hurry makes us hurt.

Whatever the pace, time will keep it and there's no outrunning it, only speeding it up and pounding the feet harder; the minutes pound faster too. Race for more and you'll snag on time and leak empty. Hurry always empties a soul.

In a world with cows to buy and fields to see and work to do, in the beep and blink of the twenty-first century, with its "live in the moment" buzz phrase that none of the whirl-weary seem to know how to do, who actually knows how to take time and live with soul and body and God all in sync?

Life is so urgent it necessitates living slow.

It's only the amateurs—and this I have been, and it's been ugly —who think slow and urgent are contradictory, opposite poles. Is this the secret that all the life experts know? That in Christ, urgent means slow. That in Christ, the most urgent necessitates a slow and steady reverence. That in Christ, time is not running out. This day is not a sieve, losing time. In Christ, we fill—gaining time.

We stand on the brink of eternity. So there is enough time. Time to breathe deep and time to see real. Time to laugh long, time to give God glory and to rest deep and to sing joy. And just enough time in a day not to feel hounded, pressed, driven, or wild to get it all done. There is time to grab the jacket off the hook and time to go out to all air and sky and green. And time to read and wonder and laugh with all of them in all this light.

All this time refracting in prism.

All this time that could refract in praise . . .

> *So what if we really paid attention*
> *and nickel-and-dimed life away*
> *on afternoon tag by the cedars.*
> *A string of bare toes with a stack of old books.*
> *This one lone bowl filling with morning light.*
> *Day after day, shelling out slow mindfulness*

on whatnots of amazing grace,
collecting pieces of God-glory.
This buying a bit of medicine
that cures ADD of the soul.

~

Lord, I can't fully express my gratitude for the time You've given.
So I want to spend my life really living today.

_____

_____

_____

_____

_____

_____

_____

_____

_____

_____

_____

_____

_____

_____

_____

_____

_____

_____

silk grace

... the heavens are the work of your hands ...
Like clothing you will change them
   and they will be discarded.
But you remain the same,
   and your years will never end.
The children of your servants will live in your presence ...

Psalm 102:25–28

It's a scant harvest of sweet corn this year.

The rains deluging in spring, then giving up its obsession with us come about mid-June.

From my post at the stove, out the window to the south, there the Farmer bends and bows over the cornstalks like an offering, the only way a life can reap a harvest.

The Farmer brings in cobs and the kids husk it back to kernels, to the nuggets of gold.

This takes time.

"Dad, can you tell Levi to stop going so fast?"

Joshua is cutting corn at the table under the spruce trees. Shalom is carrying the pans of corn to Hope and me at the stove. Malakai hauls and Caleb cuts too, on the far side of the table, with his own mountain of gold.

"Look—Levi's husking the cobs alright, but there are way too many hairs still left on these cobs." Joshua runs his hand over a cob, testifying.

"See all the corn silks he's left behind?" He holds his palm right open to all these hairs, blonde threads, summer's tassels.

"Levi …" The Farmer sets a stack of sun-warm cobs on the table and turns. "Just slow down—take your time on each cob. Do it well." He runs his fingers slowly across all the kernels of gold. "Just go slow —so you can get it all."

"Josh?" The Farmer leans over the table. "Watch how many kernels you're losing here." He smiles, winks. "We could all do that—slow down."

There was that sign in the yard of the Mennonites to the north: "Slow: Children at Play."

I could put a sign like that over the sink.

I blanch the next batch and there are the kernels of moments I've lost. How if I'd just gone slow, I could have multiplied all that He's given.

It's strange how the mind works.

The mind would rather fret about the future or pine over the past —so the mind can cling to its own illusion of control. But the current moment? It cannot be controlled. And what a mind can't control, it tends to discount. Brush past … over.

It's the battle plan of the enemy of the soul—to keep us blind to this current moment, the one we can't control, to keep us blind to Him, the One who controls everything.

There is that: What if instead of discounting the current moment, the uncontrollable, the simply given—what if I counted it—and on the God who controls it all?

What if all our running around is only our trying to run away from God—the great I AM, present in the present moment?

What if I woke to now and refused to hurry because I didn't want to refuse God?

What if I didn't discount this moment but counted it for what it is —God here?

It is only the present moment alone that holds the possibility of coming into the presence of God. Look around, breathe deep, enter into this one moment.

Now could be an altar. *This time* could be a tabernacle.

In God, there is no time, only eternity—or more simply, only now. His name is I AM. Here—*wherever my feet are*—is where I can love Him.

All these multiplying moments . . .

The steam curls up out of the pot like a prayer ascending and the windows fog and I can only see what is here, now.

Levi carries one cob to me, his witness, and all I can see is his smile.

The way he has slowed.

The way his hands now fill with this harvest of silk . . .

~

Lord God, forgive all running around that is merely a running away from You. Today, cause me to refuse to hurry because I don't want to refuse You. Instead of discounting the current moment, the uncontrollable, cause me to count it—and on the God who controls it all. This present moment holds the possibility of coming into Your presence—and I am slowing for the silk of now.

recognizing grace

What I mean, brothers and sisters, is that the time is short . . .
For this world in its present form is passing away.

1 Corinthians 7:29, 31

They tramp in loud and fling themselves out of their coats like cicada splitting skins, leave boots a trail of droppings.

The Tall-Girl lets the door swing loose and it slams the fingertips of Little-One and she yelps a pain dance of salty tears.

In the tussle out of a stubborn sleeve, a big brother swipes hard the head of a little brother and Small-Son wails the mad fists and there are coats and boots and books and who has time for all this *more*—more work, more mess, more stress?

I can feel my pulse quicken fierce. Entering fully into the moment can overwhelm, a river running wild. I will forget again, and again, and again.

But today I do remember. I breathe and I reel and I hold my ground and my tongue in this torrent coming down. I've staked my claim to the miracle.

I know the way to the Promised Land.

I do what I always need to do. I preach it. I preach it to the person I need to preach to the most. I preach to me. The skin's tugged hard by

the rush of time and I say it aloud in current pounding past, words
I need like water:

Calm. Haste makes waste. Life is not *an emergency. Life is brief and it is
fleeting, but it is* not *an emergency.*

I pick up a coat and thank God for the arms that can do it.

*Emergencies are sudden, unexpected events—but is anything under the sun
unexpected to God?*

I call a son back and hand him a hanger and thank God that he can
do this too.

Stay calm, enter the moment, give thanks.

I thank God for boots and we line them straight and the little hands
help.

And I can *always give thanks because an all-powerful God has all these
things*—all things—*always under control.*

I breathe deep and He preaches to me, soothing the time-frenzied
soul with the grace river in whisper.

Life is not an emergency.

I soothe the cheek of the mad-fisted child. I give thanks for that
one curl that always lies on his forehead beckoning. He lays his head
on my shoulder. I stroke his hair, wind my finger round that curl. I
can feel the heat of his cheeks. I can feel time's current in my blood
ease ... meander. For a moment, longer, I hold him—and life—and
I hold it mindfully, attentively ... thankfully.

Life at its fullest is this sensitive, detonating sphere, and it can be
carried only in the hands of the unhurried and reverential—a bubble
held in awe.

I carry the Small-Son boy to the table.

When those hungry eyes and empty tummies circle round the
table, smiles big just like their daddy's when he's eyeing something
good heaping high on a platter, they are all story and loud talk and

hardly able to restrain the waiting for the nod, and I grin it too. "You may ..."

They dive.

I watch them feast. They quiet. Taste buds savor it long. It's that same recipe my mama baked up when I was a kid, cowlicks sliding up the front of my hair, just like theirs.

The Boy-Man mumbles, his mouth sticky full. "I am not eating mine fast." His tongue licks chocolate off lip. "Wanna taste it all."

A boy takes a big bite, too big, smiles knowingly. I look around at their faces, their taste buds all alive, eyes shining delight in the sweet.

When did I stop thinking life was dessert?

Only in the slowing, the sitting down at the table, when His hands held the bread and the thanks fell from His tongue, do the open-eyed, the wide-eyed, see the Face they face. The fast have spiritually slow hearts.

It takes a full twenty minutes after your stomach is full for your brain to register satiation. How long does it take your soul to realize that your life is full?

I weigh the moment down with full attention here.

Life is dessert—too brief to hurry.

Time is not running out. This day is not a sieve, losing time. With each passing minute, each passing year, there's this deepening awareness that I am filling, *gaining* time. We stand on the brink of eternity.

The Small-Son pauses between bites, wiggles his tooth with tip of his tongue. I watch him and I smile. He sees me watching and he grins. He takes that last bite of chocolate-melt and with mouth still full of gooey good, he serenades soft, "I love you, Mom ... and all this."

And all this.

This cathedral moment, this time before it bursts.

All this.

Father, with all the gifts I count, You are filling me, giving me more time to recognize the significance of the story You are writing on these days. Cause me to see more of these beautiful cathedral moments You place in my life every day. I want to slow down today—and truly taste of Your goodness.

singing grace

*... always giving thanks for all things
in the name of our Lord Jesus Christ ...*
Ephesians 5:20 NASB

So we stand there and listen long, and neither one of us can stop smiling and I almost forget to breathe.

The frogs have returned, the frogs and their song.

Why does the trilling in the throat of a frog do this wondrous thing inside of me?

The oldest boy, he and the dog go crashing off through that worn carpet of leaves all rustling, boy and lab questing for big things.

But Littlest One and I?

We've already found it.

That sound.

A symphony of sound, trilling low and deep, fills the spaces between the trees, lifts us too. It is like the water, a looking glass of trunks and limbs, like the water itself croons.

With the everyday eyes I can't see the singers at all. It takes time for eyes to adjust to stillness, and only the slow really see.

Then—there they are, on the far side. *There!* These glinting eyes flickering up through waters. The peepers are back, and we can see them, see the source of the song. Who doesn't want front-row seats to glory?

Can we pick our way across the swamp—can we get any closer?

She squeezes my hand tight and we splash across the bog and in a flash, the pond snaps shut.

All is soundless. Just this glassy reflection of maple branches pointing up to that curve of muted moon come early.

She and I swish-swash farther out, as far as we can go. Then wait.

On this isle of tangled grass, the water slowly rises up to our boot ankles. A red-tailed hawk swoops and soars, his wings motionless on the currents. The moon rides higher, tailing sun dipping. We say nothing, this Little One and I, but watch the swamp's mirror, waiting stock-still for the singers to surface.

The dog, loud and large, charges up, smashing our reflection of anticipation.

"Go, Boaz," she whispers too loud at the dog. "We're waiting for the frogs to sing!"

From within the woods somewhere, a brother whistles, and Boaz ricochets off.

We wait. Then one by one, they pop to the light. We catch our breath. Dare not move.

Tentatively it comes, this chorus, then crescendo, throaty yet gilded, and she squeezes my hand and we're spellbound, smiling silly.

I could sit here forever, listening.

Doesn't all the hurry make us hurt?

Slow never killed time. It's the rushing and racing, the trying to catch up, this is what kills time—ourselves.

Why in the world do we keep wounding ourselves?

Life is not an emergency.

And this, this is the only way to slow down time . . .

Long, so very long, she and I, we just sit. We just soak in frog songs

on golden pond. When our toes are cold and the shadows stretch,
I stand slow, not wanting to.

"We leaving the frogs, now?" she whispers up to me.

I nod ... reluctant.

So Littlest One, she swings round and two splashing steps into it,
all falls quiet.

The sudden hush turns our heads.

The swamp's soundless, blinked silent by hurried sloshing.

I scoop up one wide-eyed little girl and whisper into her the ways
of God:

"You can only hear your life sing—when you still."

Father God, You tell me to still. For the very best of reasons. So today—
I will. I've been missing the songs far too long.

ugly grace

For God was pleased to have all his fullness dwell in him,
and through him to reconcile to himself all things.

Colossians 1:19 – 20

The wrinkled man in the wheelchair with the legs wrapped, the girl
with her face punctured deep with the teeth marks of a dog, the mess
of this world, and I *see.*

In German, it's *hübsch-hässlich.* In French, *d'un beau affreux.* What
the impressionist painter Paul Gauguin encapsulated as, "*Le laid peut
être beau*" — the ugly can be beautiful.

The *ugly-beautiful.*

And I nod it soft. *Yes, Father, You long to transfigure all, no matter how
long it takes. You long to transfigure all.*

In Christian circles, we elevate what we deem beautiful, endeavor
to create spheres of pristine beauty, and perhaps rightly so, for
"whatever is good, pure, lovely, think on these things." But I wonder
if maybe in the upside-down kingdom of God, what we regard as
unlovely is, in Jesus, lovely. Because somewhere, underneath the
grime of this broken world, everything has the radiant fingerprints of
God on it. Seeing the world with Jesus' eyes, we have the astonishing
opportunity to daily love the unlovely into loveliness.

And, funny thing, I'm discovering that when I lean deep into my secrets, when I draw the lens up close to the ugly in my life, examining the weave, the texture, the shadows, it too is beautiful.

When I deeply see:

- bedsheets painted with highlighter?... *children live here!*
- dead rose left too long in vase?... *lingering memories of a brother's gift.*
- Great-grandma's wicker laundry basket overflowing in the mudroom?... *we had a full, rich weekend!*
- vehicle souvenirs—a collection of shoes, Sunday school paper, Lego pieces?... *we'll gather them up too.*
- study table spread out with thoughts and ideas?... *we're thinking now.*
- a pile of tossed shoes on a shelf in the garage?... *worn days of a good summer.*
- stack of tattered books?... *stories that have become real.*

Aren't these ugly things, in their own way, part of the gift list too?

God is always good and we are always loved ... even when what He gives may appear ugly.

Up close, touching the unexpected comeliness in these domestic messes, I can't help but wonder ...

Does all the ugliness in my life look this beautiful?

It would, if I got closer.

Is that why God stays so close to us?

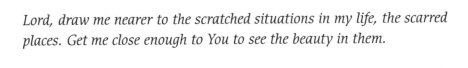

Lord, draw me nearer to the scratched situations in my life, the scarred places. Get me close enough to You to see the beauty in them.

graffiti grace

Fear not, for I have redeemed you;
I have called you by name, you are mine. . . .
Because you are precious in my eyes, and honored,
and I love you, I give men in return for you,
peoples in exchange for your life.

Isaiah 43:1, 4 ESV

When I find out what a teenager's done, I'd like to ring one slender neck. Dirt rings the mudroom sink like nasty vandalism.

To-do lists keep scrawling ugly, longer and longer. I can't find my watch anywhere. The bathroom mirror is splattered and smudged.

The weather forecast makes it impossible to know if we should plant our next field or wait until the next rain or what to do. We watch the sky for a sign. We pray, *we pray these begging prayers.*

I go a whole week watchless, not knowing what time it is.

I can't make sense of anything and this lump in my throat burns.

A high school friend, one who knew the thick glasses and the crush on the Dutch farm boy and the blessed scent of the library stacks, she and I are an impossible twenty years older and we go for a walk.

I listen to her talk of career changes and photography and marriage maybe someday soon? She has all these questions of her own. I can only nod.

We're walking down a side street in town when I stop. I stop and reach for my camera.

Rachel—she keeps talking about mortgage rates, about the Gospels and Jesus and speech pathology and the meaning of life, and her mind has always been this mushrooming wonder holding me rapt.

I aim the camera at the sidewalk. Fiddle for the shutter. The lens works to focus.

And Rachel stops midsentence. She reads the words chalked on asphalt out loud, words I'm focusing on. She reads them slow, like a decoding of everything.

"Hey beautiful, you are loved ☺" scrawled right there on the sidewalk, happy face chalked there grinning too.

"Oh." She says it like an awakening. "And here I just thought it was graffiti."

I nod in the middle of an epiphany.

The graffiti can be grace.

What seems a defacement may be a glimpse of His face. *All the writing on the wall could be love notes.*

I turn to Rachel, the camera, the capturing, still in hand, and the wind gusts, and I cheer it into the wind, into her—

"Hey beautiful, you are loved!"

And she laughs loud and we're carried.

Everything could make sense. And the real mystery of grace is that it always arrives in time. Like the wind, grace finds us wherever we are and won't leave us however we were found.

I take another picture. So I'll remember.

"This deciphers everything, doesn't it?" I say it to myself, only half asking. The other half of me knowing with a certainty I've not felt before. Love always deciphers everything.

And the dialect of God is the day just as it comes—and whenever I slow down and shift perspective, it's possible to read the impossible: the divine language of love written on all the walls. This smiling, startling alphabet of grace.

That's what jolts me, right there on the sidewalk: Grace isn't a mere Pollyanna feeling. It's a force. It's a powerful force. As startling as the power of electricity. Grace is the power of God pulsating with this passionate love of God, this jolting, blazing, dangerous love that pierces all of humanity's pitch-black.

Grace always shocks.

Grace always stuns.

Grace is always what we need.

It's what everyone groping around lost in the dark has to know: turn toward grace and you turn on all the lights. The whole black asphalt at our feet torches with the revelation.

And there is more than enough light to see it.

How the day's fresh mercies make even here clean enough.

Clean enough for all these chalkings of His love.

~⁀⁀⁀⁀

Lord God, there will be walls I run into today, walls that seem to box me in, walls that have writing on them that I long to decode. When I rightly read Your Word, I can rightly read the world: the graffiti of this world is grace in Your hands.

coded grace

I have learned how to be content with whatever I have.
I know how to live on almost nothing or with everything.
I have learned the secret of living in every situation,
whether it is with a full stomach or empty, with plenty or little.

Philippians 4:11 – 12 NLT

Sitting there before the window, I'm struck.

All these years I was saved. I had said my yes to God, but I was really living the no.

I may have always known that change takes real intentionality, like a woman bent over her garden beds every day with a spade and the determined will to grow up something good to strengthen the heart.

I may even have known that change requires more than merely thinking the warm and fuzzy thoughts about a door and a way through and that Greek word, *eucharisteo*, holding the mystery to the full life and ever after.

But none of that at all meant that I knew what to do.

To live—at all—I needed to know.

I begin the list. Not of gifts I want, but of gifts I *already have*. That is the beginning, and I smile. I can't believe how I smile. I mean, they are just the common things, and maybe I don't even know they are gifts, really, until I write them down and see what they look like.

Writing the list, it makes me feel ... happy. All day. I can hardly believe how it does that, that running stream of consciousness, river I drink from and am quenched in, a surging stream of grace and it's wild how it sweeps me away. And I add one more to the list. To feel it all again. I can't understand why it does that. And yet ... too ... the list, it feels foreign, strange. Long, I am a woman who speaks but one language, the language of the fall—discontentment and self-condemnation, the critical eye and the never satisfied.

This thanks that I am doing—it seems so ... crude. Trivial. If this list is the learning of the language of *eucharisteo*—this feels like ... guttural groanings. But perhaps the "full of grace" vocabulary begins haltingly, simply, like a child, thankful for the childlike.

But doesn't the kingdom of heaven belong to such as these?

At first, it's the dare that keeps me going. That and how happy it makes me—giddy—this list-writing of all that is good and pure and lovely and beautiful. But what keeps me going is what I read in that Bible lying open on my prayer bench looking out the window to the snow fort. The fort with a door in the wall. It's Paul writing his letter to the Philippians. I read the fourth chapter. I almost don't see it, but Paul repeats it twice in only two sentences, so I don't miss it.

There it is—the secret to living joy in every situation, the full life of *eucharisteo*. Twice Paul whispers it: "I have learned ..." Learned. I would have to learn *eucharisteo*. Learn *eucharisteo*—learn it to live fully. Learn it like I know my skin, my face, the words on the end of my tongue. Like I know my own name. Learn how to be thankful whether empty or full. Could the list teach me even that hard language? Over time?

I want the hunt, the long sleuth, the careful piecing together. To learn how to be grateful and happy, whether hands full or hands empty. That is a secret worth spending a life on learning.

I wake the next morning and I grip my pen, ink, to crack the code.

God, so many days have dialects I don't understand. How in the world do I learn the language of joy? One can only crack the code of contentment by learning the language of Your love. Let me count the ways.

naming grace

He brought them to the man to see what he would name them;
and whatever the man called each living creature, that was its name.
Genesis 2:19–20

My list of naming God-gifts lies open on the counter . . .

117. Washing the warm eggs
118. Crackle in fireplace
119. Still-warm cookies

Naming is Edenic.

I name gifts and go back to the Garden and God in the beginning who first speaks a name and lets that which is come into existence. This naming is how the first emptiness of space fills: the naming of light and land and sky. The first man's first task is to name. Adam completes creation with his Maker through the act of naming creatures, releasing the land from chaos, from the teeming, indefinable mass. I am seeing it too, in the journal, in the face of the Farmer: naming offers the gift of recognition. When I name moments— string out laundry and name-pray, thank You, Lord, for bedsheets in billowing winds, for fluff of sparrow landing on line, sun winter warm, and one last leaf still hanging in the orchard—I am Adam and I discover my meaning and God's, and to name is to learn the language of Paradise. This naming work never ends for all the children of Adam. Naming to find an identity, our identity, God's.

It's late, and in the lamplight when the bones finally rest, I read and turn a page and run unexpected into these words:

> Now, in the Bible a name ... reveals the very essence of a thing, or rather its essence as God's gift.... To name a thing is to manifest the meaning and value God gave it, to know it as coming from God and to know its place and function within the cosmos created by God. To name a thing, in other words, is to bless God for it and in it.[13]

I read the words again. The heart palpitates hard. I don't hear the clock or the slosh hum of the dishwasher. All I can see, think, is that my whim writing of one thousand gratitudes, the naming of the moments—this is truly a holy work.

This naming really *does* call now a gift, a gift of God. I read again: "To name a thing is to manifest the meaning and value God gave it." I look at a day, a thing, an event in front of me, and it may look manna-strange: "What is it?" But when I name it, the naming of it manifests its meaning: to know it comes from God. *This is gift!* Naming is to know a thing's function in the cosmos—to name is to *solve mystery*.

In naming that which is right before me, that which I'd otherwise miss, the invisible becomes visible.

The space that spans my inner emptiness fills in the naming.

I name. And I know the face I face.

God's! God is in the details; God is in the moment. God is in all that blurs by in a life—even hurts in a life.

GOD!

How can I not name? Naming these moments may change the ugly names I call myself.

I put a pen to a journal, to name solve, and I shake it when it runs dry, trace circles, and I coax out ink.

Lord, help me in the true work You've assigned to me today: to name the graces You give me this day. Cause me to name the ways You love—so I can own my own name: Beloved.

praying grace

I thank and praise you, God of my ancestors:
You have given me wisdom and power.

Daniel 2:23

I must never be deceived by the simplicity of *eucharisteo* and penning
His love list. Frogs. Sun. Journal. Naming. Love. Here. It all feels
startlingly hallowed and I breathe shallow. I should take my shoes off.

This is the other side where Daniel, man of prayer, lived. You
know, change agent Daniel, mover and shaker Daniel, second-to-
the-king Daniel, sleeping-in-perfect-peace-in-the-den-of-the-lions
Daniel. And Daniel is a man of power prayer, not because he bends
the stiff knees and makes petitions of the High Throne three times
daily. Rather, his prayers move kings and lion jaws because Daniel "got
down on his knees and prayed, *giving thanks* to his God, just as he had
done before" (Daniel 6:10, emphasis added). Three times a day, Daniel
prayed *thanksgiving* for the everyday common, for the God-love spilling
forth from the God-heart at the center of all.

I am bell and He is sure wind, and He moves and I am rung and
I know it for what it is: The only real prayers are the ones mouthed
with thankful lips. Because gratitude ushers us into the other side of
prayer, into the heart of the God-love, and all power to change the
world resides here in His love. Prayer, *to be prayer*, to have any power

to change anything, must first speak thanks: "In every situation, by prayer and petition, *with thanksgiving*, present your requests to God" (Philippians 4:6, emphasis added). "*First*, I tell you to pray for all people, asking God for what they need and *being thankful to him*" (1 Timothy 2:1 NCV, emphasis added). Prayer without ceasing is only possible in a life of continual thanks. How did I ever think there was another way to enter into His courts but with thanksgiving?

The gift list *is* thinking upon His goodness—and this, *this* pleases Him most! *And* most profits my own soul, and I am beginning, only beginning, to know it. If clinging to His goodness is the highest form of prayer, then this seeing His goodness with a pen, with a shutter, with a word of thanks, these really are the most sacred acts conceivable. The ones anyone can conceive, anywhere, in the midst of anything.

I am struck, a bell, and I chime long. Daniel is only a man of prayer because he is a man of thanks, and the only way to be a man or woman of prayer is to *be a man or woman of thanks*. And not sporadic, general thanks, but three times a day *eucharisteo*.

When I give thanks for the seemingly microscopic, I make a place for God to grow within me. This, *this*, makes me full, and I "magnify him with thanksgiving" (Psalm 69:30 KJV), and God enters the world. What will a life magnify? The world's stress cracks, the grubbiness of a day, all that is wholly wrong and terribly busted? Or God?

The list is *God's* list, the pulse of His love—the love that thrums on the other side of our prayers. And I see it now for what this really is, this dare to write down one thousand things I love. It really is a dare to name all the ways that *God* loves me. The true Love Dare. To move into His presence and listen to His love unending and know the grace uncontainable. This is the vault of the miracles. The only thing that can change us, can change the world, is this—His love.

"My soul doth magnify the Lord" (Luke 1:46 KJV).

So might I; yes, and even here.

Lord, You are the Giver infinitely greater than the sum of all gifts and how can I not slow and bow? Bow right now in worship. Kneel throughout the day in gratitude. Slow, wherever I am, in adoration. Could the miracle of becoming a person of prayer begin with just two words: "Thank You"?

all-here grace

Sacrifice thank offerings to God,
fulfill your vows to the Most High ...
Those who sacrifice thank offerings honor me.
Psalm 50:14, 23

Science may explain mechanics, but how do the eyes of the soul see?

I seize the pen on the sill and I can record another one. With my hand still dribbling dishes, with the breath all caught, I etch it down in that journal always lying out flat.

362. *Suds ... all color in sun*

I lay down the pen. Dry my hands on the dishtowel, dab at water spots transfusing into ink.

The house is a mess.

I wash up undone on an island of quiet. The loud and blur of the morning ache across my shoulders. The washing machine works, and the porcelain dove, the one with "peace" scrolled deep into wing, hangs by one clear thread. From the sink, I can see her spin, spin, this way, then that, around and around and dizzy around.

This is the way I have lived. From the time the alarm first rings and I stir on our pillows touching, stretch over his bare back and check those relentless hands keeping time on that clock. The time, always the time, I'm an amateur trying to beat time. The six kids rouse. We race.

The barn ... and hurry. The breakfast ... *and hurry.* The books, the binders ... and hurry! In a world addicted to speed, I blur the moments into one unholy smear.

I have done it. I do it still. Hands of the clock whip hard. So I push hard and I bark hard and I fall hard and when their wide eyes brim sadness and their chins tremble weak, I am weary, and I am the thin clear skin, reflecting their fatigue, about to burst, my eyes glistening their same sheer pain.

The hurry makes us hurt.

And maybe it is the hurt that drives us on? For all our frenzied running seemingly toward something, could it be that we are in fact fleeing—desperate to escape pain that pursues?

I speak it to God: I don't really want *more* time; I just want *enough* time, time to do my one life well.

The wonder right in the middle of the sink. Looking for it like this. I lay the palm under water and I raise my hand with the membrane of a life span of moments. In the light the sheerness of bubble shimmers. Bands of garnet, cobalt, flowing luminous.

I see through to the pattern. I see. The way my life, vapor, is shaping. I hadn't noticed.

Time is a relentless river. It rages on, a respecter of no one. And this, this is the only way to slow time: When I fully enter time's swift current, enter into the current moment with the weight of all my attention, I slow the torrent with the weight of me all here. When I'm looking for the glimpse of glory, I slow and enter. And time slows.

The bubble in my hand quavers, a rainbow at fringes.

And blind eyes see: It's this sleuthing for the glory that slows a life. In this space of time and sphere, I am attentive, aware, accepting the whole of the moment, weighing it down with me all here.

Full attention fills the empty ache.

Forgive me, Father, for not being all here. When Your very name is I AM
*and You are in the present and here is where I can love You. Today, when
I race ahead—return me to all here.*

hammering grace

Seek and you will find;
knock and the door will be opened to you . . .
Therefore, everyone who hears these words of mine
and puts them into practice
is like a wise man who built his house on the rock.

Matthew 7:7, 24

A contemporary and admirer of Martin Luther said, "A nail is driven
out by another nail; habit is overcome by habit."[14] When I read this
thought, I am surprised because I had never known, and I am sad for
all that would have changed if only I had.

Do not disdain the small. The whole of the life—even the hard—
is made up of the minute parts, and if I miss the infinitesimals, I miss
the whole. There is a way to live the big of giving thanks in all things.
It is this: to give thanks in this one small thing. The moments will
add up.

I too had read it often, the oft-quoted verse: "And give thanks for
everything to God the Father in the name of our Lord Jesus Christ"
(Ephesians 5:20 NLT). And I too would nod and say straight-faced,
"I'm thankful for everything." But in this counting gifts, to one
thousand, more, I discover that slapping a sloppy brush of thanksgiving
over everything in my life leaves me deeply thankful for very few

things in my life. A lifetime of sermons on "thanks in all things" and the shelves sagging with books on these things and I testify: Life-changing gratitude does not fasten to a life unless nailed through with one very specific nail at a time.

Little nails and a steady hammer can rebuild a life.

Eucharisteo precedes the miracle.

I look down at the pen. This pen — this is nothing less than the driving of nails. Nails driving out my habits of discontent and driving in my habit of *eucharisteo*. I'm hammering in nails to pound out nails, ugly nails that Satan has pierced through the world, my heart. It starts to unfold, light in the dark, a door opening up, how all these years it's been utterly pointless to try to wrench out the spikes of discontent. Because that habit of discontentment can only be driven out by hammering in one iron sharper. The sleek pin of gratitude.

I hammer.

How much is my tongue, tail of the heart, learning the real language of *eucharisteo*? I forget Eden and naming and nails, and it all seems just a bit ... juvenile. Contrived. This is the whole of the secret learning? I confess, even after all that I've seen and tasted and touched, I do scoff. I yearn for the stuff of saints, the hard language, the fluency of thanksgiving in all, even the ugliest and most heartbreaking. I want the very fullest life. I wonder, even just an inkling — is this but a ridiculous experiment? Some days, ones with laundry and kids and dishes in sink, it is hard to think that the insulting ordinariness of this truly teaches the full mystery of the all most important, *eucharisteo*. It's so frustratingly common — it's offensive.

Driving nails into a life always is.

I pick up the journal. Paul had twice said it and I mustn't forget it. He said he had to learn. And learning requires practice — sometimes even mind-numbing practice. C. S. Lewis said it too, to a man looking for fullest life: "If you think of this world as a place intended simply for our happiness, you find it quite intolerable: think of it as a place of training and correction and it's not so bad."[15] It might even be good. So I too can be like our children and the everyday training, memorizing of the Latin paradigms with the practicing chants: *amo, amas, amat*. The washing machine dings and I light up. This is why I had never really learned the language of "thanks in all things"! Though pastors preached it, I still came home and griped on. I had never practiced. Practiced until it became the second nature, the first skin. Practice is the hardest part of learning, and training is the essence of transformation.

Practice, practice, practice. Hammer. Hammer. Hammer.

This training might prove to be the hardest of my life.

It just might save my life.

Lord God, Your Son took the ringing of the hammer and the pounding of the nails to buy my salvation. Right now I offer You up my open hands. Drive out the nails of habitual grumbling with the nails of habitual gratitude. I long to be fixed to You.

awakening grace

Give thanks in all circumstances;
for this is God's will for you in Christ Jesus.

1 Thessalonians 5:18

How could I have been dead all day and not really know it?

There had been the plugged toilet, there was no getting around knowing that. We all knew that needed attention, a toilet in a house of eight always requiring immediate resurrection.

After that, there had been the mad dash to music lessons. Lots of frantic movement, sure, and yes, flailing—but really? I'd been numbed right through, just going through the motions.

And after that, there was the burnt soup, just because I failed to stir. Is that why we die in a thousand ways every day? Because we fail to stand near the heat and stir ourselves awake?

It wasn't till our littlest, Shalom, pulled those two kitties into her arms that I knew something in me had been the walking dead all day, something in me opened wide. The way those bundles of fur purr deep into the crook of her arm, so quiet. She turns to them and laughs, so full of life, and something stirs in me, so loud.

Maybe it's the way her tendrils fell that made me see it—that I had fallen asleep all day to the glory, and everywhere. That I had missed my life because I had missed the graces, and I didn't want to live like this, and isn't that what Robert Louis Stevenson had written?

"The man who forgets to be thankful has fallen asleep in life."[16]

The toilet fail, the music fumbling, the soup founder—a woman can forget in a thousand ways.

Our youngest, she says it tickles, the way his tail flicks her nose. She says it and her eyes, they laugh with all this light.

She tilts her head so the kitten is in the crook of her neck, tail waving happy—and the way she half smiles, it upholds everything. And this purring. It's all so perfectly loud.

She's tickling me awake. A heart can murmur gratitude with its every wide-awake beat.

I have known it, and I know it again, the love crawling all up and over her: intentionally look for ways to give thanks, purpose to give thanks, dare yourself to give thanks anyways—and it's the setting of an alarm and you could wake up to nothing less than your life.

Set out a gratitude list and there it goes again: an alarm set off by the startling grace of God. Giving thanks, this is an awakening—the breath of God upon the face, close and warm.

When we fill the kitty dish, you can hear it, how they drink. Our girl lies right on her tummy so she can listen.

"Hear them, Mama?" Her eyes dance indigo sky, all uncontained, all alive.

This is what we are doing—she and I smiling over spilled milk anyways.

She and I waking up ... this lapping up of life.

⌒

Father, Awaker of the dead, awaken me again today. Tendrils of Your grace will fall today—cause me not to forget to give thanks so I don't fall asleep to my life. To the whole earth spilling over with Your glory.

all-is-well grace

Then God opened her eyes
and she saw a well of water.
Genesis 21:19

Hagar and her boy were dying of thirst with a well less than a bowshot away. How to find God in the mess?

> *We [actually] saw His glory ... For out of His fullness (abundance) we have all received* [all had a share and we were all supplied with] one grace after another and spiritual blessing upon spiritual blessing and even favor upon favor and *gift [heaped] upon gift*. (John 1:14, 16 AMP, emphasis added)

That's the mystery map to the deep seeing! We saw His glory ... *because* ... we have all received one grace after another. We *have* all received one grace after another, but we only recognize the glory of God in this moment *when we wake to the one grace after another.* "If you want to be really alert to seeing Jesus' divine beauty, his glory ... *then make sure you tune your senses to see his grace*," urges theologian John Piper (emphasis added). "That's what his glory is full of."[17] Grace—*that* is what the full life is full of, what the God-glory is full of. To see the glory, name the graces. Retune the impaired senses to sense the Spirit, to see the grace. Couldn't I do that anywhere?

Why is it so hard? Practice, practice.

What insanity compels me to shrivel up when there is joy's water to be had here? In this wilderness, I keep circling back to this: I'm blind to joy's well every time I really don't want it. *The well is always there.* And I *choose* not to see it. Don't I really want joy? Don't I *really* want the fullest life? For all my yearning for joy, longing for joy, begging for joy —is the bald truth that I prefer the empty dark?

Why do I lunge for control instead of joy? Is it somehow more perversely satisfying to flex control's muscle? Ah—*power*—like Satan. Do I think Jesus-grace too impotent to give me the full life? Isn't that the only reason I don't always swill the joy? If the startling truth is that I don't really want joy, there's a far worse truth. If I am rejecting the joy that is hidden somewhere deep in this moment, am I not ultimately rejecting God? Whenever I am blind to joy's well, isn't it because I don't believe in God's care? That God cares enough about me to always offer me joy's water, wherever I am, regardless of circumstance. But if I don't believe God cares, if I don't want or seek the joy He definitely offers somewhere in this moment—I don't want God.

In His presence is fullness of joy. *He is in this moment.*

The well is always here. God is always here—*precisely because He* does *care.*

God faithfully provides water for His people everywhere.

When you know you're Hagar and you finally come to the end of yourself and all the water in your canteen is gone and you *know* you and your son are going to *die* if you don't get some joy to the lips and down the parched throat—and now; when you can no longer stand to see those you love *die* all around you from your emptiness, pray with the eyes wide open and prayer becomes revelation. Eyes change and what we see changes in them.

You have to want to see the well before you can drink from it. You have to want to see joy, God in the moment.

Thereafter, Hagar used another name to refer to the LORD, who had spoken to her. She said, "You are the God who sees me." She also said, "Have I truly seen the One who sees me?" So that well was named Beer-lahai-roi (which means "well of the Living One who sees me").

Genesis 16:13–14 NLT

Hagar had known God sees, for she had met Him before, needy in the sands, yet when sent away the second time, Hagar had forgotten. She had laid her son down to die and couldn't see any well. In the domestic cloud of dust and family, I too can forget the One who sees me, but in *eucharisteo* I remember. I cup hands and all the world is water.

Love is not blind; love is the holy vision.

For a glancing moment, I am Hagar healed, Hagar who had spoken once before in a desert exile. The well, it is still there.

There is always a well—all is well.

Lord, that You would give one grace after another—tune my senses to see Your grace. Focus my sight to see the well—that all is well.

curative grace

Then the LORD told him,
"Make a replica of a poisonous snake and attach it to a pole.
All who are bitten will live if they simply look at it!"
So Moses made a snake out of bronze and attached it to a pole.
Then anyone who was bitten by a snake
could look at the bronze snake and be healed!
Numbers 21:8 – 9 NLT

Faith is the seeing eyes that find the gauze to heaven torn through; that, slow to witness the silent weight, feel the gold glory bar heavy in palm, no matter the outer appearance. Seeing is the spiritual life: "they might see with their eyes, hear with their ears, understand with their hearts, and return and be healed" (Isaiah 6:10 NASB). "Looking comes first," wrote C. S. Lewis.[18]

First the eyes. Always first, the inner eyes.

Looking is the love. Looking is evidence of the believing.

I remember reading it only weeks before, sitting in the surgeon's waiting room with Levi, the hospital renovation progressing slowly, the patients healing only slightly faster. (Transfiguration can be the long miracle.) Levi had daydreamed out the waiting room window, listened to the stories of car accidents and work injuries from the bandaged, and I had held my book. I'd read how the Israelites looked about and saw much to bemoan, much to complain about: "They spoke against God and against Moses, and said, 'Why have you brought us up out of Egypt to die here in the wilderness? There is no bread! There is no water! And we detest this miserable food!'" (Numbers 21:5).

I had looked around at the wounded all waiting. I had turned back to the page. And what does God send the ingrates? What came to the ingrates in the Eden beginning? A slithering blanket of snakes that coil around the complaints of the Israelites, open wide and pierce the flesh with the fang. Always, ingratitude makes the poison course.

The cure against the bite of thanklessness.

The remedy is in the retina.

How we behold determines if we hold joy. Behold glory and be held by God.

How we look determines how we live ... *if* we live.

And I had read how Jesus says, "In the same way that Moses lifted the serpent in the desert so people could have something to see and then believe, it is necessary for the Son of Man to be lifted up—and everyone who looks up to him, trusting and expectant, will gain a real life, eternal life" (John 3:14–15 MSG). I had looked up from my book and into the face of a boy with his ear bandaged and I didn't want to imagine what had happened.

I had tried to take it in. Isn't Jesus Himself saying that people need to see and then believe—that looking and believing are the same thing? That in the right inner looking we can gain the right outer life ... the *saved full* life?

I had read it and had forgotten (always!), but I remember it now. "Faith is the gaze of a soul upon a saving God."[19]

Faith is in the gaze of a soul. Faith is the seeing soul's eyes upon a saving God.

That's what makes us persevere through a life: to see Him who is invisible!

Lord, You heal every infirmity. Heal my stunted sight. Open the eyes of my heart. I long to see Your heart—even when I can't see Your hand. The remedy is in the retina.

perceiving grace

"Your eyes are windows into your body.
If you open your eyes wide in wonder and belief,
your body fills up with light.
If you live squinty-eyed in greed and distrust,
your body is a dank cellar.
If you pull the blinds on your windows,
what a dark life you will have!"
Matthew 6:22–23 MSG

How do we converse with a God who may not seem to honor our honor?

In the quiet, I wonder, cue card with a memory verse in hand—if I had the perspective of the whole, perhaps I'd see it? That which seems evil, is it a cloud to bring rain, to bring a greater good to the *whole* of the world? Who would ever know the greater graces of comfort and perseverance, mercy and forgiveness, patience and courage, if no shadows fell over a life? I dare flip the cue card over and I make out words on the back side, "See now that I, I am He, and there is no god besides Me; It is I who put to death and give life. I have wounded and it is I who heal" (Deuteronomy 32:39 NASB). I nod. I know. *I know.* And these truth words reconfigure the battlefield under my feet.

I grip the card and I know all our days are struggle and warfare

(Job 14:14) and the spirit-to-spirit combat I endlessly wage with Satan is this ferocious thrash for joy. He sneers at all the things that seem to have gone hideously mad in this sin-drunk world, and I gasp to say God is good.

The liar defiantly scrawls his graffiti across God's glory, and I heave to enjoy God ... and Satan strangles and I whiten knuckles to grasp real Truth and fix that beast to the floor.

It's just that the eyes are bad—my perspective. "Your eye is a lamp that provides light for your body," Jesus said. "When your eye is good, your whole body is filled with light. But when your eye is bad, your whole body is filled with darkness. And if the light you think you have is actually darkness, how deep that darkness is!" (Matthew 6:22–23 NLT). If Satan can keep my eyes from the Word, my eyesight is too poor to read light—to fill with light. Bad eyes fill with darkness so heavy the soul aches because empty is never truly empty; empty is only a full, deepening darkness. So this is what it is to be. Eve in the Garden, Satan's hiss tickling the ear. "Did God actually say ...?" (Genesis 3:1 ESV).

No Scripture glasses to read what God is trying to write through a prodigal child? Scrawl my own quick editing on the half-finished story: *failure*. Satan's tongue darts.

Not wearing a biblical lens to decipher the meaning of a doctor's ominous diagnosis? Just read Satan's slippery interpretation: *cheated*.

Not using anything to bend the light of this world so I can read my own messy days? Spray on another layer of graffiti: *worthless*.

So I have been ambushed.

Without God's Word as a lens, the world warps.

Who deserves any grace?

When I realize that it is not God who is in my debt but I who am in His great debt, then doesn't *all* become gift?

Lord, You are the only lens that can correct the vision of a life. And if I don't hunger daily for the bread of Your Word, I'll develop sight deficiency. Make me Word reflective — that I may have the right perspective.

hunting grace

My cup overflows.
Surely your goodness and love will follow me
   all the days of my life,
and I will dwell in the house of the LORD forever.

Psalm 23:5 – 6

I don't think of it then.

Not then, when I raise my hands up in what isn't—well—in what it isn't, precisely, praise. Because really, the way I threw my hands up, it was more this lift of lament and exhausted surrender and end-of-the-day fatigue than any semblance of praise.

And I can't say it occurred to me right then either, throwing my hands up in the air, that it really could be that we were born with two hands because we never stop weighing the good against the bad, today against yesterday—and that I'm weighing everything all the time.

But I do know that the piles and the weeds and the to-do lists and the messiness of living—it can weigh right heavy and I can feel it in the shoulders, the back, the heart.

I can only say I thought of it after the weekly ceremony of looking for beauty to fill the vases, the crocks that have become furniture—permanent furniture—since spring, and the peonies.

Before, when a child brought in a fistful of Queen Anne's lace, summer's scattered doilies, it was only then I'd slip a vase off the shelf.

Or when boys raced in with first profusion of wild daffodils from the ditches . . .

Or when the Farmer would stop the tractor at the edge of the side road on the way home from the other farms, right there by the neighbor's, and he'd fill his arms with tiger lilies growing free under the maples, him feeling no shame in greased and manly hands picking slender stems, carrying flowers home for his bride.

I'd only get a vase down then.

Because it went like this:

Have beauty.

Must get a vessel.

But when Farmer gave me these four crocks, all thrift store finds, the world spun a bit differently.

So I made these vases furniture, vases that always remained out: one on the dining room table, one by the sink, one by the hearth, one in the study—permanent fixtures in a house that could be wired for glory.

So it could go like this:

Have vessel.

Now must find beauty.

Empty containers can make us seekers, hunters of glory. I need to find grace-beauty to fill the emptiness. Not bought beauty—only beauty that can be bought with attention.

A wildflower from the roadside. A branch from the woods, grasses growing long in the ditches, zinnias from the garden, a happy round face from the sunflower patch, a flowering chive or two.

"Can I gather the flowers this week?" a son asks after the weekly cleaning, hand on the back doorknob, scissors in hand.

"Can I go too?" A little girl's already flash of blond light across kitchen.

We've become this motley tribe of beauty hunters.

So, it's when I have a vase in my hand and those black-eyed Susans are long-necked and lovely that I just plunk the bouquet of flowers directly down on the antique weight scale.

It's when the levered beam falls with a clunk.

It's only then, when the beam in my own eye falls away, that I see clear what all saints must already know . . .

For those who can see, the world's beauty outweighs its burdens, its grace greater than its grime.

There is always this: pots and pans and peels. I forget to put a load of laundry in before we sit down to the dinner. I haven't taken in the load out on the line. I have to gather strewn books and take out the recycling and find a hoe for that garden.

What will I look for, to outweigh everything? *Who* will I look to, to outweigh everything?

And in the midst, my gratitude journal lies open.

It used to be that I offered generic thanks—mumble a bit of thanks before the sleep, give thanks before the meal.

Have grace.

Must give thanks—sorta (now and then).

But when gratitude journals became my permanent life furniture, white spaces opened wide, empty pages like cups to heaven, waiting to be filled with the color of His graces . . . something in me shifted.

What will I look for, to outweigh everything? *Who* will I look to, to outweigh everything?

Have space to give thanks, space to chronicle a thousand gifts.

Now must *find grace.*

I become a seeker, a looker. A God-hunter—making this a daily

82

ceremony, the gathering of grace, joy to fill the emptiness, Father-glory that never fades.

And when I look out at sunflowers, with all those sprouting weeds at their feet, I can tell just by the way they're nodding their crowning heads—the way all these flowers agree, agree.

They agree with the antique scale and here with these people in the midst of our piles.

When I go looking for glimpses of Him, when I seek to fill the empty places with more of Him who is beauty, my equilibrium recalibrates to find its center in the Judge who became grace to bestow grace and I can rightly read the scale, feel it inside, and know it's true:

If you can really see—the weight of Glory always tips the scales for joy.

I think of this, the next time I raise my hands in happy thanks . . .

How light I feel—this perfect weight.

Lord God, You are the Hound of heaven who hunts the lost down and captures us with grace. Today, make me the hound of now who hunts for glory and captures joy with just that one word: Thanks.

beautiful grace

One thing I ask from the LORD,
    this only do I seek:
that I may dwell in the house of the LORD
    all the days of my life,
to gaze on the beauty of the LORD
    and to seek him in his temple.

Psalm 27:4

Bowed at the edge of the world, Jesus asks me soft what He asked of the man born blind: "What do you want Me to do for you?"

Jesus, I am struggling and I get turned around, but I think I know, at least in part, what I want. If I had never run, if I had never fallen here, I am not sure I would have known with blazing clarity. I may not know all that it means, but this is what I want.

I whisper with the blind beggar, "Lord, I want to see" (Luke 18:41).

This kingdom laden with glory, this, the pearl of great price, the field I'd sell everything to possess. This is the pearl that crams me with a happiness that throbs, serrated edge, pit open wide for more of His glory.

Beauty, God Himself, is the voice endlessly calling and so we see. So we reach. Doubt the philosophies, doubt the prophecies, doubt the Pharisees (especially the ones seen in mirrors), but who can doubt this

—Beauty Himself? Beauty requires no justification, no explanation; it simply is and transcends. See beauty and we know it in the marrow, even if we have no words for it: Someone is behind it. Beauty Himself completes.

This is what I'm famished for: more of the God-glory.

The only place we have to come before we die is the place of seeing God.

What is this that I feel sitting here, coursing through me relentless, hot, ardent? I *have* to seek God-beauty. Because isn't my internal circuitry wired to seek out something worthy of worship? Every moment I live, I live bowed to something. And if I don't see God, I'll bow down before something else.

How could I have forgotten how badly I wanted this?

To bow down and rightly worship.

Do I have eyes to see it is His glory and not the thing?

I am bowed like wheat, raised like grass blades, grounded and rooted to now, and from Him and through Him and to Him are all things and all is His and everything that has breath praises Him, and I whisper it again, again, again, remembering, remembering, remembering.

Eucharisteo, eucharisteo, eucharisteo.

When the purity of Jesus lies over a heart, His transparency burns the cataracts off the soul. The only way to see God manifested in the world around is with the eyes of Jesus within.

God within is the One seeing God without. God is both the object of my seeing and the subject who does the act of all real seeing, the Word lens the inner eye wears.

To sit in the theater of God and see His glory crack the dark, to open the eyes of my heart to see the fountain of His grace—thousands of gifts—I have to split heart open to more and more of Jesus.

Who can split open the eyelids but Jesus? Christ Himself tears the veil to the Holy of Holies, gives me the only seeing I have.

I have been lost and now I am found and I sing it softly, before the flying of the flocks south: "Be thou my vision, O Lord of my heart . . ."

These heavy glory-waters endlessly flood from Him and God spills. Skirts of stars swirl through black space and waterfalls canter over stones, manes of runaway horses, and lone mushroom tilts in the shadows of soundless forest, and God sees it all. This is His endless experience because this is who He is—beauty overflowing. God is happiest of all.

Joy is God's life.

Don't I yearn for it to be mine?

I was lost but now am found again, Jesus, and I know what I want: to see deeply, to thank deeply, to feel joy deeply. How my eyes see, perspective, is my key to enter into His gates. I can only do so with thanksgiving. Living in His presence is fullness of joy—and seeing shows the way in.

Our endless desires are fulfilled in endless God.

I long to know Beauty, breathe it into lungs, feel it heavy on skin. To beat on the door of the universe, pound the chest of God with the psalmist: "One thing I ask from the LORD, this only do I seek: . . . all the days of my life, to gaze on the beauty of the LORD and to seek him in his temple" (Psalm 27:4).

Faith is the gaze of the soul and I want to *see in*. So I can *enter in.* Isn't that what C. S. Lewis knew too?

What more, you may ask, do we want? Ah, but we want so much more—something the books on aesthetics take little notice of. But the poets . . . know all about it. We do not want merely to see beauty, though, God knows, even that is bounty enough. We want something else which can hardly be put into words—to be united with the beauty we see, to pass into it, to receive it into ourselves, to bathe in it, to become part of it.[20]

Isn't the longing for Beauty Himself the happiest place of all?

~⌒

Lord, in Christ You name me Beloved One, and in love I call You Beautiful One. Today, turn me from seeing burdens to seeking beauty. Cause me to glimpse at the grittiness and gaze on Your glory—because could there be more joy than adoring You more?

bridge grace

Give thanks to him who alone does mighty miracles.
His faithful love endures forever.
Psalm 136:4 NLT

Count blessings and discover who can be counted on.

Isn't that what had been happening, quite unexpectedly? This living a lifestyle of intentional gratitude became an unintentional test in the trustworthiness of God—and in counting blessings, I stumbled on the way out of fear.

Can God be counted on? Count blessings and find out how many of His bridges have already held.

Had I not trusted all these years because I had not counted?

I glance back in the mirror to the concrete bridge, the one I've boldly driven straight across without second thought, and I see truth reflecting back at me: Every time fear freezes and worry writhes, every time I surrender to stress, aren't I advertising the unreliability of God? That I really don't believe? But if I'm grateful to the Bridge Builder for the crossing of a million strong bridges, thankful for a million faithful moments, my life speaks my beliefs and I trust Him again.

I fearlessly cross the next bridge.

I shake my head at the blinding wonder of it: Trust is the bridge from yesterday to tomorrow, built with planks of thanks. Remembering frames up gratitude. Gratitude lays out the planks of trust. I can walk the planks—from known to unknown—and know: He holds.

I could walk unafraid.

Is that why the Israelites kept recounting their past—to trust God for their future? Remembering is an act of thanksgiving, a way of thanksgiving, this turn of the heart over time's shoulder to see all the long way His arms have carried. Gratitude is not only the memories of our heart; gratitude is a memory of God's heart and to thank is to remember God.

I had read it this morning as I prayed the Psalms, the psalmist giving thanks for the memories. In memory, the shape of God's yesterday-heart emerges and assures of God's now-heart and reassures of His sure beat tomorrow. And for the first time I see why the Israelites are covenanted with God to be a people who remember with thanks. It is thanksgiving that shapes a theology of trust, and the Israelites bear witness and I see.

Isn't this what ultimately Jesus asks of us in the Last Supper? One of the very last directives He offers to His disciples, the one of supreme import but one I too often neglect—to remember. *Do this in remembrance of Me.* Remember and give thanks.

This is the crux of Christianity: to remember and give thanks, *eucharisteo.*

Why? Why is remembering and giving thanks the core of the Christ-faith?

Because remembering with thanks is what causes us to trust—to really believe.

Lord God, I claim Christ as my bridge back to You and I trust the Bridge Builder to hold all the moments of my life — and me. Remind me today, Lord, to give thanks to You for always holding. I am relieved of the burdens when I've believed in the Bridge Builder.

hard grace

I want to know Christ—
yes, to know the power of his resurrection
and participation in his sufferings,
becoming like him in his death.

Philippians 3:10

I can't keep myself from saying it to God, this raw sob echoing that of Teresa of Avila: "If this is how You treat Your friends, no wonder You have so few!"[21] Can I be that honest?

I am David lamenting, "Why, LORD . . . ?" (Psalm 10:1). Why this broken world punched through with losses? "How long, LORD?" (Psalm 13:1). How long until every baby thrives and all children sleep down the hall from a mom and dad wrapped up in love, and each womb swells with vigorous life, and every single cancer clinic sits empty and we all grow old together? How long?

I know a neighboring Mennonite woman folding away the clothes of her dead son, and I sit in a room full of the battered and busted and I lament: *Please*. And He takes the empty hands and draws me close to the thrum of Love. You may suffer loss but in Me is anything ever lost, really? Isn't everything that belongs to Christ also yours? Loved ones lost still belong to Him—then aren't they still yours? Do I not own the cattle on a thousand hills; everything? Aren't then all provisions, in Christ also yours? If you haven't lost Christ, child, nothing is ever lost. Remember, "through many tribulations we must enter the kingdom of God" (Acts 14:22 NASB).

The dark can give birth to life; suffering can deliver grace.

If all the work of transfiguring the ugly into the beautiful pleases God, *it is a work of beauty*. Is there *anything* in this world that is truly ugly? That is curse?

Can I believe the gospel, that God is patiently transfiguring all the notes of my life into the song of His Son?

What in the world, in all this world, is grace?

I can say it certain now: *All is grace*.

I see through the woods of the world: *God is always good and I am always loved*.

God is always good and I am always loved.

Everything is eucharisteo.

Because *eucharisteo* is how Jesus, at the Last Supper, showed us to transfigure all things—take the pain that is given, give thanks for it, and transform it into a joy that fulfills all emptiness. I have glimpsed it: *This, the hard eucharisteo*. The *hard* discipline to lean into the ugly and whisper thanks to transfigure it into beauty. The *hard* discipline to give thanks for all things at all times because He is all good. The *hard* discipline to number the griefs as grace because as the surgeon would cut open my son's finger to heal him, so God chooses to cut into my ungrateful heart to make me whole.

All is grace only *because all can transfigure*.

I take to heart the words of Thomas Aquinas, who defined beauty as *id quod visum placet*—beauty as that which being seen, pleases.

I wear the lens of the Word and all the world transfigures into the Beauty of Christ.

Everything could be eucharisteo.

Lord of Life, when I am between a rock and a hard place, cause me to know it full well: You make all grace because You transfigure all. Cause me today to believe, right in the midst of hard things, that You are patiently transfiguring all the notes of my life into the song of Your Son. Today, let me do hard things: live the hard discipline to give thanks in hard things. Today, I lean hard on You—who softens my heart.

this-moment grace

The life of mortals is like grass,
   they flourish like a flower of the field ...
But from everlasting to everlasting
   the LORD's love is with those who fear him,
   and his righteousness with their children's children.

Psalm 103:15, 17

It falls unexpected in October.

A snow-white whisper hushing the trees burnt all red.

She stands at the window and I watch it fall behind her, her at the glass and the flakes so soundless, heaven on white wing.

And I don't expect it, in a room full of women and flashing laughter, the way she turns and says it quiet—

"My daughter is dying."

Sometimes grace is the way a moment unfurls into wing and something of God flutters near.

I step closer, step in, try to catch all this falling down.

Is there really anything to murmur except to just come close and stand with someone?

She says it straight out and clear. "There have been gifts."

That when the diagnosis came, the doctor said terminal and only a year more, at the most five—but then the unexpected, this wild grace of ten whole years.

How she once sang like a bird, twirled in her four-year-old spin, and then the years of slow regression, the walking giving way to the wheelchair, the songs giving way to loss of words, and now, giving way to infant beginnings.

"It's kept us always living just in this moment—because we know today is the last like this." Sometimes you know you will never forget the way the light burns in someone's eyes.

She's a flame in snow.

"Just always so grateful for every moment we've been given." It's falling straight down behind her.

I reach out, just to touch her shoulder, and she's radiant and the truth lands here in the open hands: Giving thanks to God is what ushers one into the very presence of God. And this is why He asks us to always give thanks.

He comes to those with the open, grateful hands.

In the morning the white-laced water begins its melt, these days all vapor.

Her testament, it remains, and I remember the way she flashed grace in snow, one fading moment after another, and I want to burn thanks right into me.

In the morning light coming up from the east, it's clear— everything hanging on the trees, all that is left, all the leaves ...

Still all in this open flame of bare, ardent praise ...

~⁀

God, today is the last like this. This place, this people, this moment— it will never again be just like this. Cause my eyes to see everything in my life afresh. I may not pass by here again. Now is not a forever grace, but amazing grace.

small grace

"Truly I tell you, unless you change and become like little children,
you will never enter the kingdom of heaven.
Therefore, whoever takes the lowly position of this child
is the greatest in the kingdom of heaven."

Matthew 18:3 – 4

Her laughter makes me laugh too, and I can hear her going through the house, flagrantly recording all time and space. Child and mother, we've exchanged places, and I try to return order to chaos and she too returns to Eden, naming each moment with a frame.

Eventually, she comes looking for me, her face filled with lens, her every step activating another click. I'm separating whites from darks in the laundry room.

"Can you show them back to me now?" She holds the camera out to me, as long as the neck strap will allow. Nothing can restrain her giddiness.

Settling into a pile of laundry, our heads lean toward each other and touch. Her arm around my neck, we scroll through her photos on the glowing screen. A picture of me bent over her, showing her which button to press. I'm mountain over her lens. I can feel the laughter rising up in her, and she cups her hand over her mouth to catch the bubbling pleasure. She's enchanted by her photos. I grin.

Frame of a table. A doorknob. A bookshelf skewed on a tilt.

Yet her photos surprise, every single one. Why? It takes me a moment to make sense of it.

It's the vantage point.

At thirty-six inches, her angle is unfamiliar to me and utterly captivating: the study ceiling arches like a dome, her bed a floating barge. The stairs plunge like a gorge.

She's Alice in Wonderland, all the world grown Everestlike around and above her.

"Do you like them, Mama?" She pats my cheek with her laughter-drenched hand.

I can only murmur, flicking through her gallery. "Marvelous ... just marvelous."

She giggles and who can resist and I lay the camera aside and tickle her soft belly and she throws the head back, bliss, and I kiss blind all up that sweet neck of hers and she laughs breathless and we roll happy. And when she scampers off into other majestic realms, I look after her longing, longing to go too.

Could I?

I want that kind of crazy, happy joy, God. How to see the world again through those eyes? To live in the wide-eyed wonder of a world that unwraps itself grandiose and larger than life, so otherworldly?

As G. K. Chesterton wrote, "How much larger your life would be if your self could become smaller in it."[22]

When I stand before immensity that heightens my smallness, I have never felt sadness. Only burgeoning wonder.

Dear Lord, make me decrease that You may increase and keep me small and humble. Cause me to embrace that simplest of truths— that all wonder and worship can only grow out of smallness.

humble grace

God blesses those who are humble,
for they will inherit the whole earth.
Matthew 5:5 NLT

I'm standing in a mudroom, sorting children's dribbled shirts, grass-stained jeans. I live in laundry. How to be Little-One in now's wonderland, in Kingdom of Heaven coming? How to *live* in a state of awe when life is mundane and ordinary? I know layers of the *eucharisteo* answer because I have felt the miracle — but there are layers I don't yet understand.

Light falls in gold bars across laundry.

The watch on my wrist chimes the hour, modern bells to prayer. I stop the spinning thoughts, the probing questions, the hands sorting, the laundry work, because God needs knees more than hands. Bowed like Daniel, I move to the other side of prayer with on-the-hour prayers of thanks.

Thank You, Lord, for the perspective of a child ...

Thank You for door frames and doorknobs ...

Thank You for soaring ceilings and bed barges and tables that loom large ...

For her laughter and her wonder and her eyes that turn the world inside out and stretch it large and leave me again in surprise ... in awe ...

I murmur *eucharisteo* thanks in a pile of laundry and the world expands and heightens and deepens and surges with the glory of God, and I can feel the body decreasing and the soul increasing and joy filling the breadth between. This, *this* is like a child happily capturing pixels, our daughter giddily grasping the ball—the perspective of smallness that cultivates surprised wonder, that grows gratitude, that yields joy. The orb awe of a moon that makes the eyes see, the kaleidoscope of a bubble that makes the time slow, this is *eucharisteo* working its change on a life, but here, isn't this here another layer of *eucharisteo*? *Eucharisteo* makes the knees the vantage point of a life. I shake my head, my quiet laughter remembering her glee, because isn't that how children live? Life as a large surprise. A child has no expectations ... *A rolling ball? Surprise! A laughing aunt? Surprise! Again and again? Surprise!*

That's what a child doesn't have—this whole edifice of expectation. Without expectations, what can topple the surprising wonder of the moment?

My mama, valley wise and grief traveled, she always said, "Expectations kill relationships." And I've known expectations as a disease, like a silent killer heaping her burdens on the shoulders of a relationship until the soul bursts a pulmonary and dies. Expectations kill relationships—especially with God.

I think of it only a couple hundred times a year, that single wide-eyed night by the bed of one of our sons in the pediatric wing of a city hospital. The moaning of babes, the crying of sick children, the murmur of nurses with grim prognoses on lips and morphine in hand, these haunted through the endless hours. I did not sleep, the pain of that place begging me to pray.

After our son was given the thumbs-up and signature of release, I came home to bedrooms and bathrooms and kitchen and fridge and windows and unmerited, luxurious health and I threw up my arms in relieved gratitude.

Here? This place? Surprise!

I was a woman who saw what her life could well have been. And things but forty-eight hours earlier I entirely took for granted — even rather half resented as flawed and less than — I spun around: *All surprising grace!* And there has not been a single night the nearly ten years since, that my son and I haven't whispered in bedside prayers for those who cry out in the dark, for we witnessed and we remember and we will always carry ...

Is it only when our lives are emptied that we're surprised by how truly full our lives were?

Instead of filling with expectations, the joy-filled expect nothing — and are filled. This breath! This oak tree! This daisy! This work! This sky! These people! This place! *This day! Surprise!*

C. S. Lewis said he was "surprised by joy." Perhaps there is no way to discover joy but as surprise? This, the way the small live. Every day.

Yes, the small even have a biblical nomenclature. Doesn't God call them the *humble*?

The *humble* live surprised. The *humble* live by joy.

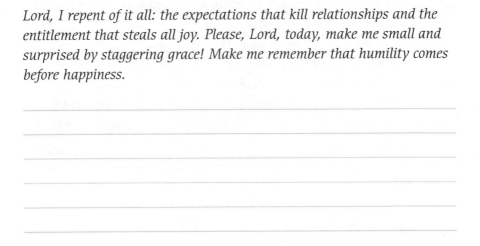

Lord, I repent of it all: the expectations that kill relationships and the entitlement that steals all joy. Please, Lord, today, make me small and surprised by staggering grace! Make me remember that humility comes before happiness.

seed grace

"Behold I have given you every plant yielding seed
that is on the face of the earth,
and every tree with seed in its fruit.
You shall have them for food."
Genesis 1:29 ESV

The two girls, they kneel in dirt, their heads near touching, and their laughter, it could be like the song of the seraphim. The dog's running in the wheat field behind the garden, gold dog breaking through green. I sort seed packets, all rattling promise. And every single one of the kids, they're all startling grimy, dirt ringing eyes like raccoons, what picking stones across the bean fields all day can do to the face, the hands, the bent back.

Now in the evening, to the bare garden, us weary and hopeful. Only one of us has shoes on. It's all a bit laughable. Bohemian. But the holy ground, isn't it always where we least expect it? I know, it's just this ...

Tomatoes at twilight. Spinach seeds. All these dirty bare feet, all their voices and ribbing and laughter. But I can feel it too, a tattered reverence ...

"Just gentle." Hope shows Shalom how to cradle the root ball of tomatoes. Do I tell the girls their rows aren't farmer straight?

"Don't drop any of the seeds." Levi leans over Caleb's shoulder.

There is light edging Caleb's knees, all his work, his gritty pants, the very bottom of his heel. It's everywhere too, the refrain of the ragamuffins: "Holy, Holy, Holy, the whole earth is full of His glory." This is what reverberates and moves me deep, the song of the wounded and washed: Holy, Holy, Holy.

"Joshua, can you bring another spade?" I call to him across the lane, him coming out of the barn, coming out from feeding all the nursing sows. We're breaking the earth open and it's making something in me heal.

And I tear open up the seed packets of zucchini, and is it this too, witnessing again this Genesis giving? That again He gives the first gift He ever gave to humanity? That again He gives the impossible gift and asks for wild faith? The seeds, they fall into my hand small, jewels. I am holding seeds, first gift He ever bestowed upon His people. Maybe this is why the bare feet? But to look at seeds and believe He will feed us? When what He gives doesn't look like near enough. When it looks like less than a handful instead of a plateful, a year full, a life full. When it looks inedible.

These seeds, they are food? It looks like a bit of a joke.

To hand someone seeds for his swelling, panging starvation, and ask him to believe in a feast—is this what everyday faith is?

Behold! For those who have learned to see—He gives, He gifts. He gifts with seeds as small as moments, grace upon grace, and the unlikely here and now, it shall sustain you, feed you. Do not disdain the small. The promise of feast is within the moments. Our enough is always in the now, because He never leaves us.

Joshua, he brings me a spade. He begins on one long row of lettuce. I plant gladioli bulbs. Levi scratches out his lines of sweet corn. Shalom pours her watering can careful over tomatoes that Hope's tucking into earth. Caleb hills up for pumpkins. We're all just ragamuffins out here hunched over our wild song of faith: *Holy, Holy, Holy . . .* We pray bent not only in sanctuary but in soil, and we bow over rows, not only in pews. And if prayers are what we seed and Cross–love is what we knead, what we reap and what we eat is the harvest of God. He is enough.

Shalom, she pours the water.

The trickle making song, making clean.

This trickle making feast.

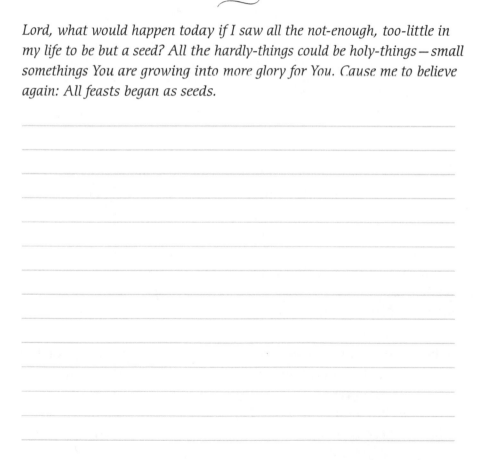

Lord, what would happen today if I saw all the not-enough, too-little in my life to be but a seed? All the hardly-things could be holy-things—small somethings You are growing into more glory for You. Cause me to believe again: All feasts began as seeds.

transplanting grace

He who was seated on the throne said,
"I am making everything new!"
Revelation 21:5

July twilight and my brother shows up at the back door.

My brother. All man. Still boy. Still freckles. Still that grin tugging at me.

"So." He rubs his hands like he's about to pull the past out of nothing. "Ya got time for a walk down the back lane?"

Shalom is already pulling at his hand, pulling hard for the back door. John and I used to go slooping up through the back ditch looking for sun-bellied frogs, and we built a base camp at the foot of the bald beech at the wood's edge and he's only a whisker younger, twelve months, thirteen days, but far older than me in adventure and spontaneity. We've come the whole long way together, a lifetime of Julys and slippery love that got away and an unexpected base of grace.

Malakai bikes ahead of us. Shalom never lets go of John's hand. The light dips the world gold and I try to open the aperture of the mind wide to snap the moment in memory. John's all talk of our Father, the first and forever One, and how he listens to Him in prayers and God leads him on in His Word. I'm right wide-open. Crazy, what wild grace can do to a guy who once boozed away everything come

Friday night. Or to an anxious girl who once twisted into a control-tight mother. Christ at the end of a cross can upend whole worlds and everything lands aright.

"There are wild raspberrrrrries back heeeeeeere!" Malakai rings the woods loud and his echo peals us happy.

We're bears rustling through undergrowth, shaking down leaves to fill hungry hands with garnet clusters hanging from canes.

If you lay a hive of raspberry red on your tongue and press your tongue right to the roof of your mouth, you can squeeze the sweet right out of every cell.

Malakai and Shalom pick and giggle, fill their mouths and pucker their lips, kissing summer's juice. John laughs. Deep and happy and up into poplars. Time can only work age into skin. Within, near the soul, time's impotent and we're forever young. I feel about eight.

"Can I pick these?" Shalom has drifted farther down the patch.

"Sure! As long as they're ripe!" Malakai doesn't even look up. Bear with a mission.

"Or do you mean those daisies, Shalom?" I step out of raspberry brambles and into the field of dreams and beans so I can see her. "You can pick all the daisies you want, sweet."

"No, those are weeds." She turns her back on the billowing clouds of delicate white and she points. "I mean these."

"Just a minute ..." The soybean leaves whisper against the bare legs and I walk all the way to her. "What do you want to pick, hon?"

"These."

I follow the direct line of her very certain index finger.
Those?

"Oh, but Shalom ..." I chuckle. "Shalom, you sure you want to pick a bouquet of those?"

She's pointing to a clump of burdock.
Burrs.

The nasty hooked balls that snag you going by, Velcro to your sleeve, tangle to your hair, knot to your pant legs, your backside, your dog. Those.

"Shalom, that's a burdock, those prickly and stickly things that get stuck in your hair, remember?"

"But they're purple, Mama." She says that word *purple* like it's jeweled, like it's royal and lush. She plucks a stem.

"I like these better than daisies, because—is white even a color, Mama?" She yanks on another stalk.

"These are all *purple*." She says that word again and it's all sugar-rich on her tongue.

Malakai's got a handful of wild raspberries and Shalom's wandering ahead with her fistful of purpled burdock, and John and I follow them through the briars of our own untamed past. Out of nothing, or the real something this is, I pull now out of what was . . .

A plant isn't a flower but a weed only by function of its place.

Transplant the weed to the heart and it blooms a flower, and I might function in this place.

Love is ridiculous and reconfigures everything.

Kai eats the raspberries before we get home and Shalom puts her burdock in a vase. At the end of a night of weeds and wild things, John and I stand at the back door grinning silly.

What is wilder than grace?

~⌒

Lord, all that I've deemed weeds in my life are only weeds by function of whether I want them in this place or not. Cause me today to transplant all my weeds into wild wonder simply by thanking You for the grace of them in this place. How else can my life bloom?

lowest grace

He must increase, but I must decrease.
John 3:30 NASB

To receive God's gifts, to live exalted and joy filled, isn't a function of straining higher, harder, doing more, carrying long the burdens of the super-Pharisees or ultra-saints. Receiving God's gifts is a gentle, simple movement of stooping lower.

> I used to think that God's gifts were on shelves one above the other, and that the taller we grew in Christian character the easier we should reach them. I find now that God's gifts are on shelves one beneath the other, and that it is not a question of growing taller but of stooping lower, and that we have to go down, always down, to get His best gifts.[23]

I knew my soul need magnify Him, but of the flesh minimizing?

And I see it then, bent over laundry, that humility isn't burden or humiliation or oppressive weight, but the only posture that can receive the wondrous grace-gifts of God—God who humbled Himself and came to the feed trough and waits to be seen in light off doorknobs and curve of vases and mound of laundry.

I shake my head, half smile, lay aside her dress because the funny thing is, the moment I try to grasp for humility, she's gone. Speak of humility, shine a light shaft on her, and she's shadow-gone in the dark. "Humility is so shy," writes Tim Keller.[24] If I focus on humility, I look inward to assess if I'm sufficiently humble and in the very act, humility darts and I'm proud, self-focused. It doesn't work. But what humbles like an extravagant gift? And hadn't I felt that joy of small child-wonder when I paused to give thanks?

The quiet song of gratitude, *eucharisteo*, lures humility out of the shadows because to receive a gift, the knees must bend humble and the hand must lie vulnerably open and the will must bow to accept whatever the Giver chooses to give.

Again, always, and always again: *eucharisteo precedes the miracle.* And you'd think I'd know that by now. But I forget. Father never forgets what I am made of, child of dust. The Wounded Warrior is achingly tender with the broken ones and He has all the patient time to gently lead those who seek and He keeps leading me back to *eucharisteo*.

Is this what is happening as I learn *eucharisteo*, to be full of grace? I humbly give God thanks for the gifts. I practice *eucharisteo*. And in that place of humble thanks, God exalts and gives more gifts and more of Himself, which humbles and lays the soul down lower. And good God responds with greater gifts of grace and even more of Himself. And I ride the undulating wave of grace, this lifting higher and higher in grace, the surging crest of joy, and this plunging lower and lower in humble thankfulness only to rise yet higher in grace.

This *eucharisteo*, it offers the ultimate joyride and I don't think I ever want to get off. Is this why the oil jars of joy never run dry but endlessly refill? He must increase, and I must decrease—not because that is burden, but so that my joy might increase with more of Him! I kneel down to toss in the laundry.

I set the dial to extra dirty. I stay on my knees and watch the water run into the washer, watch it splash against the circular glass of the washing machine's front door, hear its gurgling fall. Down it flows.

Down, always down, water runs, always looking for yet lower and lower places to flow. I watch water run and think spiritual water must flow like this ... always seeking the lowest places—and the washtub begins to rock. I must go lower. I tell myself this, watching water run. That whenever I am parched and dry, I must go lower with the water and I must kneel low in thanks.

The river of joy flows down to the lowest places.

And here on my knees I can see.

Lord God, today, lead me lower that I may be happier. Gifts are best found and received on bended knee. You are the Infinitely Good God who offers greater gifts of grace and even more of Yourself to those who humble themselves. Today, by Your grace let me ride that undulating wave of grace—going lower to find the lifting higher and higher in grace.

manna grace

He humbled you, causing you to hunger and then feeding you
with manna, which neither you nor your ancestors had known,
to teach you that man does not live on bread alone
but on every word that comes from the mouth of the LORD.

Deuteronomy 8:3

I shouldn't, but I do. I look up. Into all his hardly tamed grief.
I feel wild. My brother-in-law's eyes shimmer tears, this dazed
bewilderment, and his stoic smile cuts me right through. I see his
chin quiver. In that moment I forget the rules of this Dutch family of
reserved emotion. I grab him by the shoulders and I look straight into
those eyes, brimming. And in this scratchy half whisper, these ragged
words choke—*wail.* "If it were up to me ..." and then the words
pound, desperate and hard, *"I'd write this story differently."*

I regret the words as soon as they leave me. They seem so
un-Christian, so unaccepting—so *No, God!* I wish I could take them
back, comb out their tangled madness, dress them in their calm Sunday
best. But there they are, released and naked, raw and real, stripped of
any theological cliché, my exposed, serrated howl to the throne room.

His firstborn, Austin, had died of the same genetic disease only
eighteen months prior. Now he was about to bury his second son in
less than two years.

"You know . . ." John's voice breaks into my memory and his gaze lingers, then turns again toward the waving wheat field. "Well, even with our boys . . . I don't know why that all happened." He shrugs again. "But do I have to? . . . Who knows? I don't mention it often, but sometimes I think of that story in the Old Testament. Can't remember what book, but you know — when God gave King Hezekiah fifteen more years of life? Because he prayed for it? But if Hezekiah had died when God first intended, Manasseh would never have been born. And what does the Bible say about Manasseh? Something to the effect that Manasseh had led the Israelites to do even more evil than all the heathen nations around Israel. Think of all the evil that would have been avoided if Hezekiah had died earlier, before Manasseh was born. I am not saying anything, either way, about anything."

He's watching that sea of green rolling in winds. Then it comes slow, in a low, quiet voice that I have to strain to hear.

"Just that maybe . . . maybe you don't want to change the story, because you don't know what a different ending holds."

The words I choked out that dying, ending day echo. Pierce. There's a reason I am not writing the story and God is. He knows how it all works out, where it all leads, what it all means.

I don't.

His eyes return, knowing the past I've lived, a bit of my nightmares. "Maybe . . . I guess . . . it's accepting there are things we simply don't understand. But He does."

And I see. At least a bit more. When we find ourselves groping along, famished for more, we can choose. When we are despairing, we can choose to live as Israelites gathering manna. For forty long years, God's people daily eat manna — a substance whose name literally means "What is it?" Hungry, they choose to gather up that which is baffling. They fill on that which has no meaning. More than 14,600 days they take their daily nourishment from that which they don't comprehend. They find soul-filling in the inexplicable.

They eat the mystery.

They *eat* the mystery.

And the mystery, that which made no sense, is "like wafers of honey" on the lips.

> He gave you manna to eat in the wilderness, something your ancestors had never known, to humble and test you so that in the end it might go well with you.
>
> *Deuteronomy 8:16*

A pickup drives into the lane. I watch from the window, two brothers meeting, talking, then hand gestures mirroring each other. I think of buried babies and broken, weeping fathers over graves and a world pocked with pain and all the mysteries I have refused, refused, to let nourish me. If it were my daughter, my son? Would I really choose the manna? I only tremble, wonder. With memories of gravestones, of combing fingers through tangled hair, I wonder too . . . if the rent in the canvas of our life's backdrop, the losses that puncture our world, our own emptiness, might actually become places to see.

To see through to God.

Lord God, Maker of all, when You give manna moments, may I give You thanks for the mystery. Because the manna that makes no sense—You will make it my sustenance. Today, in all the "what is it?" moments, turn me to give thanks for who You are.

bread grace

For all the promises of God find their Yes in him.
2 Corinthians 1:20 ESV

I remember it right then, passing pig farms. And that God would bring that story to memory now.

How bread became a comfort when bombs fell in World War II, shattering earth and all that is within and children wept for parents, cried for food. Refugee camps offered beds to huddling, dirty frames but could not furnish rest. Blast of days haunted pitch of nights. Nothing comforted shell-shocked, gaunt children. Fear rimmed the eyes and the hearts pounded, too loud, and the sleep fled. I know how nights blinked with the saucer eyes, the vigilant, terrified eyes. But somewhere in the dark, up between each narrow row of beds, a hand came to pull up the thin sheets, a hand to touch each bony shoulder and offer the fear-chased something to seize.

A piece of bread.

Dazed child hands took the bread, tucked in with bread. They gave thanks and rested on pillows of trust. The bread hushed the fears with assurance: "The sun sets and He has provided and you've ate. Tomorrow the sun will rise and again He will provide. You will eat bread again."[25] Hands clutch bread. And finally it comes: the terrified sleep deep.

I shake the head; sleeping with bread, a strange mental image. And yet really ... isn't that what that gratitude journal on the counter is? Opening the hand to receive the moments. Trusting what is received to be grace. Taking it as bread. Recount how we laughed today. How we cried today and it too was grace. How He fed us. We ate. We filled. We swept up the crumbs. So He lays us down to sleep. Trust tucks in. He has blessed today. Will He not bless again tomorrow? Sleeping with bread may seem strange, but Jesus knew the wilder.

He knew I'd only trust, rest, when I lived with bread in hand. When I eat manna.

Eucharisteo, remembering with thanks, *this is the bread.*

We take the moments as bread and give thanks and *the thanks itself becomes bread*. The thanks itself nourishes. *Thanks feeds our trust.*

And it swells up in me and I can't stop it, this surging sense of emancipation. Over a steering wheel in a white pickup, I can't help this glorious laugh, the laugh of the unafraid and the bold, the giddy hope of the bread carriers, the manna eaters.

Until Home and Promised Land and complete clarity, I'm a wanderer crossing bridges, wanderer eating manna, eating mystery. For really, as long as I live, travel, is there ever anything else to eat? I either take the "what is it?" manna with thanks, eat the mystery of the moment with trust, and am nourished another day—or refuse it ... and die. Jesus calls me to surrender and there's nothing like releasing fears and falling into peace. It terrifies, true. But it exhilarates. This, this is what I've always wanted and never knew: this utter trust, this enlivening fall of surrender into safe hands.

There is no joy without trust!

I can feel all the sinews releasing, the opening of the heart chambers, the unfurling of a life into one reverberating, exultant yes!

For no matter how many promises God has made, they are "Yes" in Christ (2 Corinthians 1:20).

Yes in Christ!

To the enfleshed Yes who said yes to this moment and yes to last year's illness and yes to the cracks of my childhood and yes to the nail and yes to my name in the Book of Life, hear me say YES!

The power of sin and death and fear-sent-from-the-Enemy are forever ended because we can trust in the bridge even if it's caving, in God even when it's black, in manna nourishment even when we don't know what it is. The God whom we thank for fulfilling the promises of the past will fulfill His promises again.

In Christ, the answers to the questions of every moment are always *Yes!*

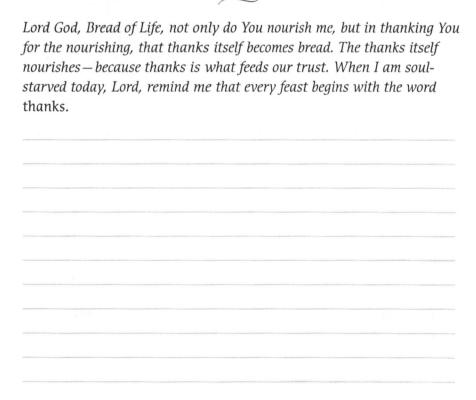

Lord God, Bread of Life, not only do You nourish me, but in thanking You for the nourishing, that thanks itself becomes bread. The thanks itself nourishes—because thanks is what feeds our trust. When I am soul-starved today, Lord, remind me that every feast begins with the word thanks.

wedded grace

"A man leaves his father and mother and is joined to his wife,
and the two are united into one." This is a great mystery,
but it is an illustration of the way Christ and the church are one.
Ephesians 5:31 – 32 NLT

When the back door of the sanctuary opens and she floats down the aisle under that veil of white, the groom grins giddy.

A son leans down the pew and whispers it too loud. "The guy looks like he's going to split, he's so happy."

The groom smiles like he's swallowed the canary through all three stanzas of the hymn they sing together. He beams deliriously when he tells us all from the platform, "I'm so grateful to the Lord that God let this day finally happen."

It looks like his cheeks might hurt, his happiness through the vows: "After my complete commitment to the Lord, I promise you will be first in my life."

The Farmer squeezes my hand. Murmurs it in my ear. "We should go home and recite our vows again too."

I turn to catch his eye. "All over again. In a heartbeat." He grins like he's twenty, winks, and pulls me all into him.

And when the preacher says the groom can kiss his bride, he fumbles nervous with the hem of the veil, too anxious to get to her, and the guests all chuckle embarrassed and when he finally cups her face in his hands and revels unabashedly in her, I look away to the floor. This is all theirs.

Afterward, at the reception, there's a little bottle of honey, liquid light in glass, on the plate of each guest. A son pats the Farmer's arm and tells him they found honey, still good, in the pyramids. That honey always lasts.

That they've given us a token of forever.

On Sunday morning, we sit in the pews of our chapel, and the preacher's preaching who we are in Christ.

"In Christ, you have immediate access to God and all of this is yours — joy, acceptance, completeness, rest, righteousness, access to the throne of God. You are sealed and He has pledged Himself to His people and you are His."

And I look around and it strikes me — Why aren't we all standing? Why aren't we all grinning giddy? Why aren't we all smiling like we just might split?

I keep reading the vows the preacher has on the screen, slow and captivated.

He's given all these gifts to all His children, no matter where we are — why not slow and really revel in this because what love is greater than this?

- *Joy is yours.* "Though you have not seen Him, you love Him, and though you do not see Him now, but believe in Him, you greatly rejoice with joy inexpressible and full of glory." *(1 Peter 1:8 NASB)*

- *Acceptance is yours.* "To the praise of the glory of his grace, wherein he hath made us accepted in the beloved." *(Ephesians 1:6 KJV)*

- *Completeness is yours.* "And in Him you have been made complete." *(Colossians 2:10 NASB)*

117

Why don't our cheeks hurt with the happiness of it all? What more could we want? How do we contain ourselves? Surely all the believers believe?

The vows of the Christ, they are covenant, and He lasts when we lose everything else and all the gifts are in Christ alone.

We could float.

On the way out of the chapel after service, I catch a glimpse of it through the stair door window, what's hanging there in the stairwell.

I step into the empty quiet of the landing, just to the read the words again, quilted there on the wall hanging.

> And I John saw the holy city, new Jerusalem, coming down from
> God out of heaven, prepared as a bride adorned for her husband ...
> And God shall wipe away all tears from their eyes; and there shall be
> no more death, neither sorrow, nor crying, neither shall there be any
> more pain: for the former things are passed away.
>
> *Revelation 21:2, 4 KJV*

The stairway's still. This is ours. Like honey, sweet to the soul and healing to the bones, all His covenant, a gift of forever.

When the Farmer asks me on the way home why I'm smiling, I squeeze his hand. Murmur something about how I just can't stop, the promises that won't let me go—all the light honey in the trees ...

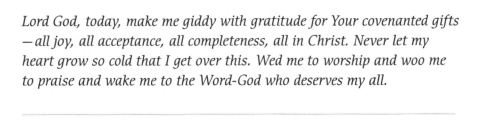

Lord God, today, make me giddy with gratitude for Your covenanted gifts —all joy, all acceptance, all completeness, all in Christ. Never let my heart grow so cold that I get over this. Wed me to worship and woo me to praise and wake me to the Word-God who deserves my all.

love song grace

I have loved you with an everlasting love;
I have drawn you with unfailing kindness.

Jeremiah 31:3

Only as the gifts are attended does God's choosing of *us* become so utterly passionate.

It's a new voice, this endless stream of grace, one I never get over. This love song He is singing, it is the antithesis of life's theme song, that refrain of rejection I know so well. That mental soundtrack of condemnation and criticism that I've let run on continuous replay, lyrics I learned from the grade-three boys huddled on the ice, exploding laughter when my skates slid east, west, and I fell south; from the trendy city girl moved to the country who snickered at my thrift store shirts; from the critical eye of every evaluator, judge, assessment, grade. That heavy beat of failure, a pounding bass of disappointment, it has pulsed through my days and I've mouthed the words, singing it to myself, memorizing the ugly lines by heart. They become the heart.

For years, I tried medication, blade, work, escape, all attempts to drown out that incessant, reverberating drum of self-rejection. All futility, acidic emptiness.

But here, I hear it well: The only thing to rip out the tape echoing self-rejection is the song of His serenade. One thousand gifts tuned me to the beat. It really is like C. S. Lewis argued—that the most fundamental thing is not *how we think of God* but rather *what God thinks of us*: "How God thinks of us is not only more important, but infinitely more important."[26] Years of Christian discipleship, Bible study, churchgoing had been about me thinking *about* God; practicing *eucharisteo* was the very first I had really considered at length what God *thought of me*—this ridiculous and relentlessly pursuing love, so bold. Everywhere, everything, Love!

Giving thanks awakens me to a God giving Himself, God giving Himself *to me*—for me—a surrender of love.

The discipline of giving thanks, of unwrapping one thousand gifts, it unwraps God's heart bare.

I choose you. Live!

He chooses His children to *fully* live! Fully live the fullest life—the astonished gratitude, the awed joy, the flying and the free.

I hear the beat of his heart, that song crystal clear: "'I have loved you,' says the LORD" (Malachi 1:2).

In a thousand ways He woos.

In a thousand ways I fall in love.

Isn't falling in love always the fullest life?

~

Oh, Lord, if You sing love over me forever, could I not sing thanks to You just for today?

one-hundred-times-a-day grace

All this is for your benefit,
so that the grace that is reaching more and more people
may cause thanksgiving to overflow to the glory of God.
2 Corinthians 4:15

Out the kitchen window the sky rolls out. Apple blossoms fill the orchard. The morning dove warms her bluing hope. I can hear Him, what He is telling the whole world and even me here: this is for you. The lover's smile in the morning, the child's laughter down the slide, the elder's eyes at eventide: this is for you. And the earth under your feet, the rain over your face upturned, the stars spinning all round you in the brazen glory: this is for you, you, you. These are for you—*gifts*—these are for you—*grace*—these are for you—*God*, so count the ways He loves, a thousand, *more, never stop*, that when you wake in the morning you can't help turn humbly to the east, unfold your hand to the heavens, and though you tremble and though you wonder, though the world is ugly, it is beautiful and you can slow and you can trust and you can receive each moment as grace. *Eucharisteo. Eucharisteo. Eucharisteo.*

And the moment opens unexpectedly. I'm in the cemetery

kneeling, tracing the only five letters carved deep in that slab of granite laid down in the dirt.

"A-I-M-E-E." *Loved one.*

I remember her silken hair. I still don't know why He took her. I don't know why her children don't run free on spring days with mine, laugh with my sister's. Don't know why my parents' hearts were left to weep, eroding all away. Though I cry, this I know: *God is always good and I am always loved* and *eucharisteo* has made me my truest self, "full of grace." Doesn't *eucharisteo* rename all God's children their truest name.

"Loved one."

Me, my dad, my mama, all the children, all the broken ones, all the world, He sings us safe with the refrain of our name, "Loved one."

In the window next to the stove, the porcelain dove soars. In the sill a framed print of Rembrandt's *Supper at Emmaus* invites. How many times a day do I look at this print in my kitchen and return to that sacred moment of soul communion in a still gallery? How many times a day do I again reach to embrace Him in communion thanks? It comes again now like it does every day, what I had read after I had already counted thousands of gifts: that this discipline of counting graces is as old as God's people themselves, the seriously devout Jews of today still giving thanks to God one hundred times a day. The words of the rabbis have been impressed deep into my skin, my being, their words beckoning the way into joy:

> Blessings keep our awareness of life's holy potential ever present. *They awaken us to our lives....* With each blessing uttered we extend the boundaries of the sacred and ritualize *our love of life. One hundred times a day, everywhere we turn, everything we touch, everyone we see.* The blessings can be whispered. No one even need hear. No one but the Holy One. *"Holy One of blessing, Your presence fills the Universe. Your presence fills me."*[27]

My gratitude journal is lying open on its permanent home on the counter, enumerating moments, making a ledger of His love. It is G. K. Chesterton who encapsulated the truth of my numbering life: "The greatest of poems is an inventory."[28] I grin happy in the midst. No, I'll never stop the counting, never cease transcribing the ballad of the world, the rhyme of His heart. He and I, a couplet. Count one thousand gifts, bless the Holy One one hundred times a day, commune with His presence filling the laundry room, the kitchen, the hospital, the graveyard, the highways and byways and workways and all the blazing starways, His presence filling me.

This is what it means to fully live.

Father God, if devout Jews thank You one hundred times a day — might I thank You one thousand times in a lifetime? Might I begin anew today? Because when we've been with You ten thousand years, we'll have no less years to sing Your thanks than when we've first begun. May my extravagant practice begin now. Bless the Lord, O my soul — because this is what blesses the soul.

numbered grace

So teach us to number our days,
That we may present to You a heart of wisdom.
Psalm 90:12 NASB

In morning light in the woods, I kneel low with a camera.

In a clearing of saplings, a friend from church smiles into the March winds. I click the shutter. She began chemo this week to contain four cancerous lumps that can't contain her mouthed thanks to God. I say, "Cheese!" and her four-year-old tilts his head and flashes his dimple. Her five children ring her like a promise.

Less than ten miles away, my sister sits in a rocking chair watching the red digits blink on an oximeter.

She's sitting there with the 24/7 monitoring of oxygen saturation levels of my niece born under heaving breath prayers. The child whose every breath reminds us to pray to YHWH, God, whose name sounds like our own breathing. For seventy-three days they have written down the numbers on the oximeter screen, high, low, of her lungs inhaling, exhaling . . . stopping.

Midafternoon in the kitchen, Hope turns at the sink and smiles at me, her with hair pulled back in a barrette and laying long down her back, her wearing my sweater but her own shoes because mine are too small now. It's only a turning, but I'm struck. Awakened to my daughter who doesn't seem a child anymore. She is twelve and she isn't. So tall and lovely. She reaches for a towel.

She's a stem of slender grass, hardly swaying in spring winds.

I murmur it. "Well, Hope — I think my days are numbered now ..."

Weren't they always? And I just don't bother keeping track?

My eyes can't leave her, taken with her so grand.

Hope dries her hands on the towel, knits her brow, confused. "Why are your days numbered?"

Numbered.

I hadn't really meant it quite like that. Not like my sister recording oxygen numbers. Not like a mother of five counting chemo days.

I half smile, only a bit tender in the upturning. "Just thinking. The days of being taller than my children are numbered now. By summer's end, you'll be looking down at your old Mama ..."

She blushes, shakes her head, that long mane of hair falling thick over her shoulders, laughing ... "Mama!"

She's elegance. Willow girl, sky eyes. I record the moment.

Numbered. Is this how He teaches?

How else to seize a heart of wisdom with your life?

Number the beats, record the blessings, enumerate the gifts, see One at the center of it all, and know there is much and it is fleeting and it is in the accounting of a life that we accumulate thanks for anything in life. This way is gone all too soon. Who keeps track to keep a heart of wisdom, to keep a perspective that keeps Him in focus?

Is it the accountants who know the full measure of His grace?

The heart of wisdom, always this accounting heart ...

Hope is bent over Shalom, Shalom with bows in her hair that Hope once wore and how much longer these ribbons of pink? I watch them and wonder if this is it:

The way to learn to number our days is to count the moments of His grace.

I don't want to miss what this all sums up to.

The children making up games about a grandmother's big toe
... and the girl-giggles shaking rocking chairs ... and the deepening
laughter of teenage boys and the robin bobbing scarlet hope across the
back lawn, a blaze, and the littlest in her striped leotards ... and sons
with widening shoulders and a brother smiling when the other walks
into this living room tumbling with jokes ... and the Farmer stealing
a sideways grin my way and him saying: "Isn't it just good medicine to
hear them all so happy?"

And her so long and lovely in my kitchen, turning and unfurling,
her one heart beating this steady mercy.

One long certain beat after one long surrendered beat ...

*Lord God, today, please make my heart an accounting heart that I
may present to You a heart of wisdom. When I count the moments of
Your grace, I number my days — and don't grow numb to Your grace.
Or my life.*

affectionate grace

And then I'll marry you for good — forever!
  I'll marry you true and proper, in love and tenderness.
Yes, I'll marry you and neither leave you nor let you go.
  You'll know me, GOD, for who I really am.

Hosea 2:19 – 20 MSG

The bride wears white.

And the day I get married I do, yet most of my life I've worn black. I know who I've been.

The first memory I ever held was the blood of my sister running, everything alive draining away. I came from here. We breathed grief. Black fears formed me.

There were years I cut myself along the thin skin of the wrists, wild for a way out of a darkness that chokes.

On a Sunday morning we sit in our country chapel. Shalom slips up on the Farmer's lap. I sit waiting, rubbing my wrist. Rubbing the edge of my black cuff. Before us are the bread and the juice of the vine. The loaf of bread that will be broken in half.

The bread will be pure white. I can never thank Him enough.

It's still in the chapel sanctuary. The piano notes begin. One woman's quavering voice begins alone.

"When I survey the wondrous cross …"

The nails right through. The glorious way out of everything that has been. Out of all my black ... the horror of death, the relentless prison of fear, the way pain pursued, a whole family aching endless with wounds we couldn't heal. Him the only Way out.

And when I survey, she's there too, way in the back of my past, Bible teacher Kay Arthur on a long-ago platform, her voice quaking with Calvary's love—it's hell and it's healing, and I'm not yet twenty-one, and when she tells me what love saved me, the spit and the beard plucked cruel, His ribs rising and falling hard, wild gasp for breath, the purest God-Man subjected to vilest humanity—all my hard exterior cracks right open and runs liquid and what do we know of true love?

"See from His head, His hands, His feet, sorrow and love flow mingled down ..."

And I'm sitting there before Communion, rubbing my wrist, and all I can think of is that woman in Luke 7, the one in the shadows with her alabaster jar and she's weeping in the black. She knows who she's been.

A dark storm, she cries. She wets Jesus' feet with her tears. She "rains," it reads, in the original Greek *brecho*. She rains; she's this *brecho* that breaks. She's this full rain falling. She's this heart-water let loose. Him so pure and His feet so dirty. Her so filthy and Him her only purity. Will anyone wash His feet with their love?

And that woman, she has no pitcher but she has passion—the kind no Pharisee could ever understand and she has no water but she has her heart.

She pours it out. *She pours it out.*

And with no towel but tresses, no hand cloth but her hair, she does the unthinkable, the scorned and the disgraced. When all Jewish women were required to keep their hair done up, lest they be seen as shameful and loose, she lets her locks down.

Rabbis, men of the law, said that if a woman loosed her hair in public, let her hair flow mingled down, it was grounds for divorce. Grounds to be shamed and sent away.

But there is a love far greater than law.

That Luke woman, she lets her hair loose, lets her love loose, and she looks loose and there are always Michals who will scorn David's dancing before the ark—but Jesus lets her kiss Him.

It seems shocking, appalling, too intimate, and this *kataphileo*, these kisses, this is the same word of the father kissing the prodigal son, a symbolic picture of God embracing, the father falling on the neck of his child and kissing, and doesn't the whole realm of earth need to be seized with a power of a great affection, "for we are members of his body, of his flesh, and of his bones" (Ephesians 5:30 KJV).

The Pharisee had no water for His feet but she gave her heart-water.

And the Pharisee had no towel but she laid out her loose, silken hair.

And the Pharisee gave no kiss but she couldn't stop kissing His feet, her grateful love the most expensive perfume—the kind that cost her the respect of men but earned her the pearl of great price, the acceptance of Jesus—"for she loved much" (Luke 7:47 ESV) ... "Your faith has saved you; go in peace" (Luke 7:50).

She gave her grateful love as an intimate gift.

And her heart-water and costly love are gifts fully received and accepted by Christ.

And our God is the God who whispers, "Call Me Husband." The God who says, "Yet you were naked and bare. Then I passed by you and saw you, and behold, you were at the time for love; so I spread My skirt over you and covered your nakedness ... and entered a covenant with you so that you became Mine" (Ezekiel 16:7–9 NASB).

The Savior celebrates communion with His bride, the spiritual oneness He made her for. Will anyone wash His feet with their love?

"Were the whole realm of nature mine, that were an offering far too small . . ."

I'm murmuring the notes of the song before Communion and these inner dark clouds split into white, the *brecho* that breaks, and Elie Wiese had said, "No one is as capable of gratitude as one who has emerged from the kingdom of night."[29]

In the middle of the hymn, Shalom leans off the Farmer's lap, leans her face into mine that's emerged from the dark, her long hair, curling wisps, framing everything and she reaches out to touch my cheek . . .

My wet cheek. I can never thank Him enough.

She who's been freed of much, freely loves, and she who knows how she's forgiven, how she gives thanks. She gives back everything. It is possible to have a form of religion and not be formed by love for Christ. And it's possible to see the law but be blind to love. And love for all, no matter what, is what never fails . . .

Who feels such gratitude for their salvation in Christ that they live such affection for Christ? Who can say just this: "Lord, you know all things; you know that I love you"? Oh please, Lord—let it be said of us.

What is greater proof to the world of the power of the gospel of Christ than the world witnessing the power of profuse love for Christ?

Shalom brushes away what's running down, all my rain, and she barely whispers it. "Why you cryin', Mama . . . and smiling?"

I have no words. Just shake my head. Just eyes on the words of the hymn.

Just love falling.

"Because of Jesus, Mama?"

I nod and the sanctuary fills:

Love so amazing, so divine, demands
my soul,
my life,
my all.

Lord, forgive me. It is possible to have a form of religion and not be formed by love for Christ. Lord, forgive me: It is possible to see the law but be blind to love. Lord, forgive me. You know all things and You know all the days I didn't thank You — that I have not expressed my love to You. Today, cause me to feel such gratitude for my salvation in Christ that I live such affection for Christ.

standing grace

No longer will violence be heard in your land,
  nor ruin or destruction within your borders;
but you will call your walls Salvation
  and your gates Praise.

Isaiah 60:18

God doesn't need us to praise Him but He needs us to praise.

What else keeps us from bitterness?

Down by the water's edge the boys build a sandcastle.

Caleb wields his shovel like a man with a back built for trenches, for getting to the bottom of things. Sand sprays and he piles.

The summer I got meningitis, I'd lain on a blanket, still, and he ran after seagulls on this beach, about in this same spot, just east of the lifeguard chair. He'd been three that summer and smelled of buttery popcorn and his laughter squealing after swooping gulls, it had gone down like a carbonated elixir. I had gotten well. He had gotten taller. Thirteen more summers and he had shed the boy skin and I watch now how he bends. How to grow up the man that's just under that boy's skin?

Levi hauls up pails of water from the shore and he pours. "See them standing over there, Mom?" He leans over his five-gallon pail and whispers it in my direction, a secret slipping down to me off a slope of freckles.

"I heard that boy say to his dad that our castle's big. Think they're watching us build, Mom?" He half turns and scoops out a handful of wet sand to gird up a sandy palisade. He already knows how it's best to just keep digging and not look to see who's watching.

Kai and Joshua, the sand dribbles straight from their fingers and it's the tips of them sculpting, grains pressed down into the grooves of who they are. The walls grow higher. They keep at it, building and forming. Or this happens — the sand settles, sinks. Crumbles. It's there on the beach — nothing stands still, the moments always moving in a direction.

And it is like that, the way the sand moves, every word moving either one way or the other — words raising Christ or building self higher.

Words praising Him or wrangling to be praised ourselves.

This seeping of bitterness or straight spires of blessings.

"I need more water, Levi — or it's going to fall." Joshua curves over his section of wall like a prayer. I'm not sure how my life stands. How my inner and outer walls stand, how I make a home. Unless we make it a habit to give thanks, we habitually give our family grief.

Unless we consistently speak praise, we consistently speak poison.

Unless we are intentional about giving God glory throughout the day, our days unintentionally give way to grumbling.

"Levi — it's crumbling over here!" Kai turns quick. He's looking beyond himself for help. It's only when we focus on the Christic center of everything that everything finds it center and walls stand. It's in praising a Savior in all things that we are we saved from discouragement in all things.

"Thanks, Levi." Kai murmurs what matters to Levi. Kai pats more sand in cracks and Levi tilts the pail and kneeling together, they bridge the gap.

"Thanks, Levi."

Does it always come down to just two ways to do life? Do doxology —or do destruction.

From here, I watch how they build their house.

How they look over their shoulder to see if it stands . . .

Father God, make me speak praise today, not poison; make me intentionally give You glory throughout the day, that my day doesn't unintentionally crumble in grumbling. In thanking You in all things, I am saved from discouragement in all things and this today is my earnest prayer: Make me do doxology, not destruction.

lonely grace

For his invisible attributes,
namely, his eternal power and divine nature,
have been clearly perceived,
ever since the creation of the world,
in the things that have been made.

Romans 1:19–21 ESV

So after dinner she picks coneflowers in the garden. Cradles the long stems in her apron skirt, carries them up through the picket gate. And she turns to me on the top step of the porch, holds her apron out to me, all those purple petals — art in an apron.

"Why is there all this loveliness?" She wants to know.

I almost tell her — the world is full of loveliness because it's full of His love.

Isn't that the meaning of beauty? The fundamental purpose of loveliness is to convey His love. Everywhere, wildflowers, even in cracks in concrete sidewalks. Everywhere, this fragrance, this pursuit, this passion.

But I don't know how to say that — when I know that coneflowers unfold off the porch and she stands there with an apron heavy with garden glory and the sunflowers nod yes, when 30,000 children have starved to death in the last 90 days in the Horn of Africa famine. That's over 330 children every single day.

Why is there all *this loveliness*?

Don't you mean — why is there famine and why is there this shocking disparity, and what is right in a world of diets and death by starvation?

But doesn't she really have a right to question it all — the sunflowers sparking in sun flare, the light falling late through the trees, all gold like this, the phlox blooming along the picket? I see that too, on the porch. The extravagant art that makes up this world, it does jockey for an answer.

The existence of loveliness everywhere, it begs explaining.

If I raise the problem of evil in this world — shouldn't she raise higher the greater problem of good? If evil is seeming evidence to eradicate God from our mental landscape, then doesn't goodness, even in this apron, testify to the gospel truth of God?

How can we behold loveliness and say that this world looks like it would if there were no God? I don't know if I have thought of this before — the great problem of good on this planet.

Augustine had asked two questions of the world: "If there is no God, why is there so much good? If there is a God, why is there so much evil?"

I wonder if I have spent a lifetime murmuring under my breath only the second question? But why don't I first get hung up on the first question? The one my girl is bringing in with the flowers — why all this loveliness and where does it come from? The great problem of good on this planet implies that there is a Great God in heaven.

Do we not wonder at the why of good because fundamentally all human beings presume the overspilling grace of God? That good is our intended atmosphere — and evil is the exception? Isn't our default to ignore the expected and focus on the unexpected?

And even our deeming anything good or evil, it betrays our deep-seated beliefs—because how can mere nature be either? Isn't it just is? To even assess events as good and evil reveals our true paradigm: We believe there is a moral center at the center of the cosmos, God at the axis of the universe.

But if there is really a God at the center of the universe, love at the core of the cosmos, love manifesting itself as loveliness in the garden —doesn't He care about the 330 children with names and dreams who lay in Somalia with flies buzzing around their listless, wasting-away limbs till they breathe their last starving breath sometime this afternoon? Yet, if I think God doesn't care about the hurting—am I not believing the chief lie of humanity? The one hissed in the Garden to Eve, the first deception that deceives us still—that God doesn't care about the needs of His children. And maybe this is why the world hemorrhages—if we think God doesn't care, why should we?

Isn't it easier to blame Him? When I believe the Edenic lie that God doesn't care—is that the excuse to turn away, to spread the lie that God doesn't care—when maybe the truth is that it's humanity that doesn't care? If we love because He first loved us ... do we now care, because we know He did first care, has always cared, will always care—and has the nail scars to definitively prove it. If all the world believed the truth of God's character—that God cares—wouldn't this world become a caring place? He cares, so we care; He loved first, so we love now. *Why is there all this loveliness?*

Do I tell her this—that there is enough loveliness, enough beauty, enough love in this world—enough food in this world—if we would just share? That the problem of evil in the world isn't a problem for proof of God—but a problem of our own turned-inward hearts? And when we turn our hearts outward, we in turn bear testimony to the loving existence of God, of the body of Christ right here ...

I pick one coneflower out of her apron, twirl it between fingers.

Do I tell her that all this loveliness does this too: All this good makes me grateful, and my own heart needs this—a filling of His great-fullness. Gratefulness is always to Someone and when I am grateful, isn't it always evidence of God—a filling with awe of His great-ness. For all this world's sureness of the benefit of gratitude, how can we then deny that there is a Benefactor?

There is never nameless gratitude, but every instance of gratitude gives away what every skeptic really believes: Every breath is a gift and if life is a gift, there is a Giver, and if there is a Giver—all's grace. When all's grace—we give, because a gift never stops being a gift to be given ...

"It's God, isn't it?—All this loveliness ..." She says it to me smiling, picking out one of the coneflowers to inhale deep, picking up the scent of God.

She didn't need me to say anything.

There are things that need no words. His love clearly manifest in the everywhere problem of good. In every coneflower curling itself into a megaphone of mercy.

This one long echo of evidence, a loveliness lingering ...

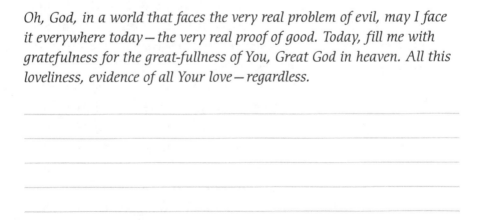

Oh, God, in a world that faces the very real problem of evil, may I face it everywhere today—the very real proof of good. Today, fill me with gratefulness for the great-fullness of You, Great God in heaven. All this loveliness, evidence of all Your love—regardless.

kindling grace

Then they cried out to the LORD in their trouble,
    and he delivered them from their distress.
He led them by a straight way
    to a city where they could settle.
Let them give thanks to the LORD for his unfailing love.

Psalm 107:6 – 8

Mama has the tea ready when I get there for prayer group and Bible study first thing in the morning.

I have on the socks that the woman with the five kids and the stage-four cancer knit for me.

This is always the first thing—to go right into the throne room of God wearing nothing less than your aching prayers.

Anne's on time for our early Saturday morning study at Mama's, sitting at the end of the living room, there in the wingback, there with her Bible long open, like a woman waiting for the Coming.

I, of course, come late. Like a foolish woman straight out of a 6:00 a.m. parable, still trying to trim her lamp, trying to remember her oil, trying to stay awake. Anne, she smiles grace, as the rain pounds steady on the windows, all the leaves coming down wet and clinging, yellow and red and sad in first gray light.

I take the seat at the end of Mama's couch. Curl my red knit socks up under me. Mama, she hands me a mug of steaming tea, apple cinnamon, and tells me it's Psalm 107 this morning and could I just read the chapter right out loud?

Read it because it's manna and you've got nothing to give if you haven't gathered and you have to gather Word-manna at daybreak if you're going to gain from it the daylong.

Read it because it's your very life and why live emaciated and I open it like a woman who needs to be cured of one wild and lifelong eating disorder. I read Psalm 107: "Let them give thanks to the LORD for his unfailing love and his wonderful deeds for mankind ..." And Anne looks over and Mama looks up and Mama asks it aloud. "Well?"

I pull at my socks and there is a lone beautiful woman battling cancer with her knitting needles and chemo and mothers grieving over children gone and men broken over everything shattered and hadn't Spurgeon said it?

> There is no greater mercy that I know of on earth than good health except it be sickness; and that has often been a greater mercy to me than health ... It is a good thing to be without a trouble; but it is a better thing to have a trouble, and know how to get grace enough to bear it.[30]

Know how to get grace enough to bear it.

It is a better thing to have a trouble, and know how to get grace enough to bear it. And we get grace enough to bear it—when we run into the arms of Grace who bore it all, into Him who is more than enough.

I run my hand across the Scripture page. Gather the manna up into hands, what really is, and all that feeds. Our cries to the Lord are what give us communion with the Lord. It's the dire distress that drives us into the deep devotion. It's when all fails, His love never fails—and this is why we are a people who can always give thanks.

The lights in the early morning, lights reflecting in the window, in the dark and in the rain—those lights look like tongues of fire.

Mama murmurs the words again. "Then they cried out to the LORD in their trouble ... Let them give thanks to the LORD." The Word open before a trio of women, it burns.

What if I gave thanks in the trouble, for the trouble, because the trouble is a gift that causes me to turn? What if I loved God not for His goods but for His love itself that is goodness enough? The theologian J. R. Miller wrote:

> Christian thanksgiving is the life of Christ in the heart—transforming the disposition and the whole character. Thanksgiving must be wrought into the life as a *habit*—before it can become a fixed and permanent quality. An occasional burst of praise, in the midst of years of complaining, is not what is required. Songs on rare, sunshiny days; and no songs when skies are cloudy—will not make a life of gratitude. The heart must learn to sing *always* ... Thanksgiving has attained its rightful place in us, only when it is part of all our days and dominates all our experiences.[31]

Mama fills our cups again with tea and the steam, it rises straight up, and I can see it in the window, the rising in burning lights. The reflection of those socks tucked up under me, the grief underlying. I drink down all this heat.

It's only when grief and grace kindle us to the very same flame of gratitude to God—it's only then that our love for God ignites in a pure blaze of glory.

It's raining so hard.

We read and pray and offer up our tenacious thanks. Close our Bibles. Carry out our manna. I pull boots on, up over those socks, and cry out and into the communion. Step out into the morning storming.

Into the leaves falling in wind, the clinging in everything streaming straight down.

All these leaves, all this amber and scarlet—all this in pure flame.

God of fire, of light, of purity and holy glory, burn me with your Word. Take my distress and make it beautiful, this opportunity for deeper communion with You. May it light a purer devotion to You in all things that come today, I pray ...

endless grace

So then, just as you received Christ Jesus as Lord,
continue to live your lives in him, rooted and built up in him,
strengthened in the faith as you were taught,
and overflowing with thankfulness . . .
and in Christ you have been brought to fullness.

Colossians 2:6 – 7, 10

Come Monday morning I forget. A child loses a book, has an exam, is late for practice. I stress over the trite, a phone call, what's for dinner, a deadline.

Am I living God's best for this life or am I bankrupting any legacy of faith? What misery lurks in the next twenty-four hours and the next? Stress can be an addiction and worry can be our lunge for control and we forget the answer to this moment.

My baby is five. She falls asleep in my arms after the close of dinner prayers, us still seated at table, and I hold her long after the Farmer has put the rest of the tribe to bed, her curls damp and etching into my skin and I don't move. Her face is turned toward mine, broad and open, eyelashes whisper of gold. I trace her lips, gentle curve of all things beautiful. The way her eyes danced today, soul light, the arch of her eyebrows and that lyrical laugh, heaven's echo that entirely undoes me. Her breath is warm on my face, all that is alive and warm and breathing inside of her now, falling upon me, and I can't capture it, hold it, this, her life now, me in this moment. She is leaving me, she's growing up and moving away from me, and she stirs and I sweep back the crop of the golden ringlets.

Stay, Little-One, stay.

Love's a deep wound and what *is* a mother without a child and why can't I hold on to now forever and her here and me here and why does time snatch away a heart I don't think mine can beat without?

Why do we all have to grow old? Why do we have to keep saying good-bye?

He soothes His own restless child in arms with the whisper, law of the universe that He's writing deep into this heart: *eucharisteo always precedes the miracle, child.*

And the chin trembles and I stroke her cheek, her body leaning back against mine, and I tentatively open the hand to receive the gift of now ... I name the now gifts and I await miracle.

That button nose. I touch a finger to its tip and smile. I gaze long, memorizing.

That sprinkling bridge of freckles. I brush my finger across them. These, these I will remember.

The way that singular curl spirals over her ear. The way it winds like silken staircase, on and on and on. And I lean over and the lips seal the delicate spot on her forehead with a long kiss, her skin berry wine and I feel Him, His kiss of tender truth:

All fear is but the notion that God's love ends.

Did you think I end, that I will not be enough?

I am infinite, child.

I wrap a thread of her curls around a finger. I stare into that face conceived in love, reflecting love, and I feel His fall soft on me. I am child in His arms and His breath falls warm upon my face and what I feel for this daughter He feels for me, and the gifts, all these gifts

I keep counting, they are His love gifts and they're slowly waking me up to the tenderest, fiercest Love of all.

Cradling this child, her eyelashes fluttering, her breath rising and falling in sure and steady rhythm, I know it in the pulsing, real, surest kind of way: "Perfect love casts out all fear." His love had done that.

The table still needs to be cleared. The bowls washed. The bread put away. Snow falls in the dark, white on a barn roof. I can't imagine what deeper layers of my wounds *eucharisteo* will gently peel back to heal, but I take her sleeping hand and trace the lines of her skin and I keep on counting blessings to keep on remembering to keep on walking out into the unknown.

I clutch a Perfect Love that knows no end.

Lord God, forgive me for raging against time's snatching away—in a thousand different ways—a heart I don't think mine can beat without. Remind me that all fear is but the notion that Your love somehow ends. You never end; our God is always infinite and enough. Today, let me walk unafraid: Your endless love ends all my fears.

losing grace

Every good and perfect gift is from above,
coming down from the Father of the heavenly lights,
who does not change like shifting shadows.

James 1:17

In the middle of a stiff winter wind she asks to go to the beach.

That's where she says she wants to celebrate the turning of her calendar year, this year's birthday. To stand on the frozen snow and turn her face directly into whatever is coming this way.

Nothing can mean nothing and everything means something. Yes —everything.

We're the only ones there. We walk the long boardwalk, our footsteps echoing hollow. She will be sixty-one this year. We stand on iced sand hemmed with white snow and she says nothing, gazing out at bared waters.

I don't ask what she's thinking. The sunlight seems paled, hardly there in the numbing cold. I watch the way her hair moves in the wind, white waves of their own.

We wander down to where the waves crash on the stones, the water breaking its way onto the unwavering sand.

Doesn't her silence say this, that this was the way to live? The water lets go again and again on the granite, this oceanic surge of song, this symphonic crescendo.

Is there anything more beautiful than the wild surrender to *the Rock?*

The song is always found in the surrender.

Mama knew there'd be days like these, when I'd see.

How many more years do I have with her to walk the winter shore? Her hair is whiter than winter and are we already in this season now?

I want spring again. I feel like the child, our shoulders touching here at the sea.

There's a whole lifetime of memories here at the lake. How many Sunday picnics of fried chicken have we had right up there at the lighthouse? She'd serve extra helpings of green coleslaw and I'd pump the swing high and I could see how we might soar straight out over the lake. There's a time when you think nothing will end.

I lean into her and she leans into me, and we're warmer like this, close. Doesn't there have to be more than a decade left of this? No, there doesn't have to be anything. The waves keep breaking. Couldn't she stay until she's 117?

When you wake to losing someone, you win love. When you realize that what you have you will lose, you win real eyes. You win grateful joy.

It comes across the water and I turn to face it directly: It's only when you realize everyone you love will one day leave you that you really begin to love. I reach over for Mama's hand and she does that, she squeezes mine softly and that says more … maybe more than anything. Maybe most.

Someday, it is possible, I could stand here on my own sixty-first. I can close my eyes and almost see that. How then she will be the memory already flown across the waters. How the song will sing on and I will hear notes that were long hers.

And the thought comes like a wave over me: *How I will miss her!*

The way to experience unlimited elation may be to imagine unexpected limitation. Imagine losing sight and open your eyes to a brighter light. No water, and the next cold glass becomes desert rain. Envision life without the loveliness of those you love—and you see how much you love.

Her half smile there in the wind, it makes me half hurt, her pure worn beauty.

There's a way to wake up and not to live numb. The way to love life is to imagine losing it. The one who loses his life finds it.

The water keeps giving away to the shore. One day all this will be gone. The sun, it seems so strong now, bright across water.

Mama, she lets the wind blow her hood right back and I don't feel numb and there is a theological term for this, all this: *Grace.*

Full-blown grace.

Standing there, she and I, we watch as it comes straight across the waters—as it comes directly this way.

Us here and alive and in awe that any of this is at all . . .

This wind awaking everything.

Father God, may I wake to losing someone today—so I can win love. Cause me to realize that someday I'll lose what I have—so I can win real eyes. Let me experience unlimited elation today—by imagining unexpected limitation. Let me envision life without the loveliness of those I love—and I can see to love more.

joyous grace

Dear brothers and sisters,
when troubles come your way,
consider it an opportunity for great joy.
James 1:2 NLT

"What in the world were you thinking? How many times have we said no running? I am just …" I'm spewing and it's ugly and the words are so frazzled with frustration they fray midstream. I can feel the slow smothering, the tight choking, and I can feel it in the throat, rising.

My knees are stiff and it's jarring, how peace can shatter faster than glass, the breakneck speeds at which I can fall—and refuse to bend the knees at all.

I look into the faces of the guilty and a son arcs his eyebrow, shrugs his shoulders, nonchalant.

I hold my head in my hands and ask it honest before God and children and my daily mess: *Can we really expect joy all the time?*

I will struggle to heed this until I am no more: "Dear brothers and sisters, when troubles come your way, consider it an opportunity for great joy" (James 1:2 NLT), and I will listen and *again* I will listen and I will wrestle to put skin on it: "Rejoice in the Lord always. I will say it again: Rejoice!" (Philippians 4:4).

I gnaw my lip. The body howls when joy is extinguished. The face shrivels pain, the voice pitches angry cry. "No man can live without joy" is what Thomas Aquinas wrote. And I confess, it is true, I have known many dead waiting to die.

The glass lies everywhere broken.

I may feel disappointment and the despair may flood high, but to *give thanks* is an action and *rejoice* is a verb and these are not mere pulsing emotions. While I may not always feel joy, God asks me to give thanks in all things because He knows that the *feeling* of joy begins in the *action* of thanksgiving.

I know it well after a day smattered with rowdiness and worn a bit ragged with bickering. Joy doesn't negate all other emotions — joy *transcends* all other emotions.

Only self can kill joy.

I'm the one doing this to me. The demanding of my own will is the singular force that smothers out joy — nothing else. Dare I ask what I think I deserve? A life with no discomfort, no inconveniences? What do I really deserve?

God does not give rights but He imparts responsibilities — response-abilities — inviting us to respond to His love-gifts. And I know and can feel it tight: I'm responding miserably to the gift of this moment. In fact, I'm refusing it. Proudly refusing to accept this moment, dismissing it as no gift at all, I refuse God. I reject God. *Why is this eucharisteo always so hard?*

I had thought joy's flame needed protecting.

My own wild desire to *protect* my joy at all costs is the exact force that *kills* my joy.

But flames need a bit of wind.

I hadn't known that joy meant dying. I can trust.

I can *let go.*

Joy — it's always obedience.

I know it deeper now: This *eucharisteo* is no game of Pollyanna but the hard edge of blade.

Only self can kill joy.

I take a long deep breath. I step from the stairs, stairs that have led all the way down into this.

I kneel down into a mess of glass.

Eucharisteo makes the knees the vantage point of a life. I bend, and the body, it says it quiet: "Thy will be done." *This* is the way a body and a mouth say thank you: *Thy will be done.* This is the way the self dies, falls into the arms of Love.

This is why. This is why the fight for joy is always so hard.

"No one who ever said to God, 'Thy will be done,' and meant it with his heart, ever failed to find joy—not just in heaven, or even down the road in the future in this world, but in this world *at that very moment*," asserts Peter Kreeft. "Every other Christian who has ever lived has found exactly the same thing in his own experience. It is an experiment that has been performed over and over again billions of times, always with the same result."[32]

I am kneeling in glass and my memories of shattered glass and Jesus comes soft— *"Thy will be done" is My own joy story, child, from beginning to end.*

And I hear it soft too, what all His life speaks: Joy is in the acquiescing.

A circle of children stand around me, watching, waiting. Long slivers of transparency, blades, lie before me, catching light.

I humbly open my hand.

Without a word, one by one, they come to the outer edges and they kneel too.

And I humbly open my hand to release my will to receive His, to accept His wind. I accept the gift of now as it is—*accept God*—for I can't be receptive to God unless I receive what He gives. Joy's light flickers, breathes, fueled by the will of God—fueled by Him.

A shaft filters through an afternoon window and the cracks of the aged wood revive in sun.

I pray.

I let go. Lay the hand open. The sun slides across old hairline scars. My palm holds light.

Lord God, You ask me to give thanks in all things today—because You know that the feeling of joy begins in the action of thanksgiving. Today, cause me to do Your will, not mine—and let me release my desire to protect my joy at all costs. Today, open my hand to joy in surrendered obedience.

pit grace

Praise the LORD, my soul,
   and forget not all his benefits—
who forgives all your sins
   and heals all your diseases,
who redeems your life from the pit
   and crowns you with love and compassion ...

Psalm 103:2 – 4

I am mad.

I'd like to will myself out of it but the blood is pounding loud in my ears and the sons slash at each other with the dagger eyes. *Why?* Can I just go back to the moon and the brazen glory? But there's always the descent from the mount. The meeting of the crowd, the complaining, the cursing.

How to be a contemplative here, seeing the fullness of God ...?

Why throw toast in your brother's face?

"*Why* would you throw that at him?" I'm too shrill, too gaped, too blind-white angry.

How do I fix this? Them? Me? In the messy, Jesus whispers, "What do you want?" and in the ugly, I cry, "I want to *see*—see You in these faces." He speaks soft, "Seek My face." I want to answer with David, "My heart says to you, 'Your face, LORD, do I seek'" (Psalm 27:8 ESV) but I'm desperate to grab someone, anyone, and shake hard, *"How do I have the holy vision in this mess?* How do I see grace, give thanks, find joy, in this sin-stinking place?"

The moon and the geese fly high, unsullied and wide-eyed, and I'm too twisted.

A boy drives a plate hard back down the table at his brother. And God tries to gently drive timeworn words from another wrestler— from the knowing of my head to the bleeding of the heart:

> You would be very ashamed if you knew what the experiences you call setbacks, upheavals, pointless disturbances, and tedious annoyances really are. You would realize that your complaints about them are nothing more nor less than blasphemies—though that never occurs to you. Nothing happens to you except by the will of God, and yet [God's] beloved children curse it because they do not know it for what it is.[33]

A blasphemer.

I pull out a chair from the table, sink down. The sunflower heads have turned low. What compels me to name these moments upheavals and annoyances instead of grace and gift? Why deprive myself of joy's oxygen? The swiftness and starkness of the answer startle. *Because you believe in the power of the pit.*

Really? I lay my head on the table. Do I really smother my own joy because I believe that anger achieves more than love? That Satan's way is more powerful, more practical, *more fulfilling* in my daily life than Jesus' way? Why else get angry? Isn't it because I think complaining, exasperation, resentment will pound me up into the full life I really want? When I choose—and it *is* a choice—to crush joy with bitterness, am I not purposefully choosing to take the way of the Prince of Darkness? Choosing the angry way of Lucifer because I think it is more effective—*more expedient*—than giving thanks?

Blasphemer. *Blasphemer.*

I rake my fingers through my hair. Who's the real sinner at breakfast on Tuesday, the one with the stinking pig in the temple?

Senses are impaired if they don't sense the Spirit and somebody, *tell me*, how do I tear open tear-swollen eyelids to see through this for what it really is?

Can I be so audacious? To expect to see God in these faces when I am the blasphemer who complains, who doesn't acknowledge this moment for Who it is?

How did Jesus do it again? He turned His eyes. "And looking up to heaven, he gave thanks and broke the loaves. Then he gave ..." (Matthew 14:19). He looked up to heaven, to see where this moment comes from. Always first the eyes, the focus. I can't leave crowds for mountaintop, daily blur for Walden Pond—but there's always the possibility of the singular vision. I remember: Contemplative simplicity isn't a matter of circumstances; it's a matter of *focus.*

I take a deep breath, say nothing to them, but I look up to heaven and I give thanks aloud, in a whisper: "Father, thank You for these two sons. Thank You for here and now. Thank You that You don't leave us in our mess."

My heart rate slows. Something hard inside softens, opens, and this thanks aloud feels mechanical. But I can feel the heart gears working. "Thank You for toast. Thank You for Cross-grace for this anger, for the hope of forgiveness and brothers and new mercies."

I look for the *ugly-beautiful*, count it as grace, transfigure the mess into joy with thanks and *eucharisteo* leaves the paper, finds way to the eyes, the lips. This, this is what Annie Dillard meant: "Seeing is of course very much a matter of verbalization. Unless I call my attention to what passes before my eyes, I simply won't see it. It is, as Ruskin says, 'not merely unnoticed, but in the full, clear sense of the word, unseen.' "[34]

I speak the unseen into seeing and I can feel it, this steady breathing in the rhythm of grace—*give thanks (in), give thanks (out)*. The eyes focus, apertures capturing Beauty in ugliness. There's a doxology of praise that splits the domestic dark.

I look over at my son tearing away at toast. Why am I a habitual reductionist? Why do I reduce God in this moment to mere annoying frustration? Why do I reduce The Greatest to the lesser instead of seeing the lesser, this mess, as reflecting The Greatest? I have to learn how to see, to look through to the Largeness behind all the smallness.

Isn't He here?

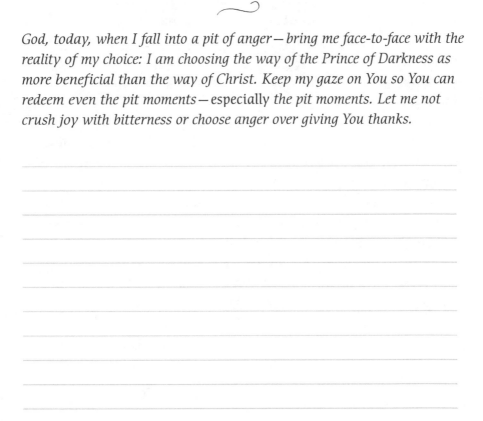

God, today, when I fall into a pit of anger—bring me face-to-face with the reality of my choice: I am choosing the way of the Prince of Darkness as more beneficial than the way of Christ. Keep my gaze on You so You can redeem even the pit moments—especially the pit moments. Let me not crush joy with bitterness or choose anger over giving You thanks.

shielding grace

Then he said to them all:
"Whoever wants to be my disciple must deny themselves
and take up their cross daily and follow me."
Luke 9:23

All the mothers around the world, around the seas rising high and the fires burning low, they all rock babies on a globe that spins on this axis of thin black letters.

We have Bibles at the table.

Pages of black letters, like long iron shafts, and around this the whole world goes around, spinning on His Story.

And I can hear it, how it turns after dinner, the children all turning Truth pages of Scripture around the table, pages skin thin, and we can see right through to the center.

This is my favorite book, Kai tells us this, clutching the Bible's leather-bound pages tight, and that smile, and he wants to read Ephesians aloud to us.

My mama turns the pages of that special edition of the Four Holy Gospels, traces the illuminated letters, the art framing the masterpiece of His expression. Mama's stilled.

After we clear the table, Levi belts his Bible right to his waist. He says this way he'll always have it close. His Bible, it looks like a shield tied to him and I want one.

Joshua, he spends Sunday afternoon reading *Unshaken*, how Haiti quaked and God never moved, and I watch how he can't stop turning the pages. Caleb says he wants to read it after Josh is done and I remember how we prayed through those days when the world seemed to implode. The Farmer calls me to come see images of Japan. I lay down my reading of Job, my book of common prayer.

I look at the pictures of Japan after the tsunami, of a curve of the planet smeared with this wave of ache, splintered wood piercing right into the earth. Women weep. Grieving can be prayer, the way we cry and know He hears.

I don't see one photo of a broken heart.

How do broken hearts mend? Do some hearts heal all wrong, all twisted and crooked and weak?

What do we make of a world that needs remaking? There's only one Crossbeam that promises a whole new world.

Only one Beam to line a heart up straight again, one Carpenter who can repair a torn-apart heart.

Levi's on the couch, reading the gospel of Matthew.

And it's here, even here, this slender pin at the center of the globe —that slides certain under the violently grinding plates and a surging ocean wall and all our fissured lives, and it's the Word of the Word-God who took the shaft and keeps His promises and names Himself the Father of the Needy.

God has done that: put the poor man on the center stage in His story of compassion for the world.

The Farmer is lingering long over this photo—a man standing with his son in the midst of a wreckage of lumber and dreams and steel.

If I am moved but choose not to respond, won't I soon harden, unable to respond?

When we are touched, we must reach out or soon we stiffen and nothing touches us and we feel nothing.

That Bible Levi is reading, it has these words, Jesus' words. "Now that you know these things ..."

Christian hands never clasp and He doesn't give gifts for gain because a gift can never stop being a gift—it is always meant to be given. When we are grateful for His gifts, we give the gifts away because a gift never stops being a gift.

How will this planet change if God's people do not become its change?

All afternoon I keep coming back to my study Bible.

I run my fingers along the Holy Writ, run my hands across the lines like groping along a ledge, looking for a crevice to grip in this world shook hard and wracked with pain.

I find it there, in His pierced-through hands ...

And I hold on.

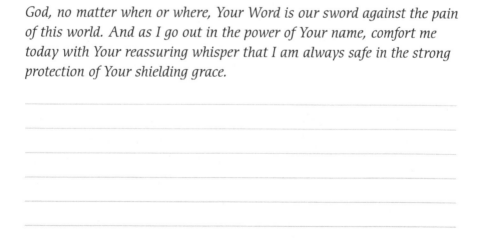

God, no matter when or where, Your Word is our sword against the pain of this world. And as I go out in the power of Your name, comfort me today with Your reassuring whisper that I am always safe in the strong protection of Your shielding grace.

full-bodied grace

"Do you understand what I have done for you?" he asked them . . .
"Now that I, your Lord and Teacher, have washed your feet,
you also should wash one another's feet."

John 13:12, 14

Jesus is about to let flesh be broken with nail, heart be broken with rejection, chains be broken with bleeding love. And in His last hours before His earthly end, He doesn't run out to buy something or catch a flight to go see something, but He wraps a towel around his waist and kneels low to take the feet of His forsakers gently in hand and wash away the grime between their toes.

This is the full-bodied *eucharisteo*, the *eucharisteo* that touches body and soul: hands and knees and feet awash in grace.

At the last, this is what will determine a fulfilling, meaningful life—a life that, behind all the facades, every one of us longs to live: gratitude for the blessings that expresses itself by *becoming the blessing*.

Eucharisteo is giving thanks for grace. But in the breaking and giving of bread, in the washing of feet, Jesus makes it clear that *eucharisteo* is, yes, more: *it is giving grace away*. *Eucharisteo* is the hand that opens to receive grace, then, with thanks, breaks the bread; that moves out into the larger circle of life and washes the feet of the world with that grace. Without the breaking and giving, without the washing of feet, *eucharisteo* isn't complete. The Communion service is only complete *in service*. Communion, by necessity, always leads us into community.

Eucharisteo means "to give thanks," and *give* is a verb, something that we do. God calls me *to do* thanks. *To give the thanks away.* That thanks-*giving* might literally become thanks-*living*. That our lives become the very blessings we have received.

I am blessed; I *can* bless. *Imagine!* I could let Him make *me* the gift! I could *be* the joy!

This is one of His miracles too—the taking of a life and making it a blessing.

Liturgy has its roots in the Greek word *leitourgia*, meaning "public work" or "public servant."

This life of washing dishes, of domestic routine, it can be something wholly different. This life of rote work, it is itself public work, a public serving—even this scrubbing of pans—and thus, if done unto God, the mundane work can become the living liturgy of the Last Supper. *I could become the blessing, live the liturgy!* I rinse pots and sing it softly, "This is my song of thanks to You ..."

In the moment of singing that one line, dedicating the work as thanks to Him, something—the miracle—happens, and every time. When service is unto people, the bones can grow weary, the frustration deep. Because, agrees Dorothy Sayers, "whenever man is made the centre of things, he becomes the storm-centre of trouble. The moment you think of serving people, you begin to have a notion that other people owe you something for your pains.... You will begin to bargain for reward, to angle for applause."[35]

When the laundry is for the dozen arms of children or the dozen legs, it's true, I think I'm due some appreciation. So comes a storm of trouble and lightning strikes joy. But when Christ is at the center, when dishes, laundry, work, is my song of thanks to Him, joy rains.

Passionately serving Christ alone makes us the loving servant to all. When the eyes of the heart focus on God, and the hands on always washing the feet of Jesus alone—the bones, they sing joy, and the work returns to its purest state: *eucharisteo*. The work becomes worship, a liturgy of thankfulness.

Father of all, make me a servant of Christ alone today, that I might be the loving servant of all, bending the knee to You to bend the knee and wash the feet of others. Today, make me know it again: eucharisteo isn't fully in my heart until I make my life about washing feet.

dark grace

In him we were also chosen,
having been predestined according to the plan
of him who works out everything in conformity
with the purpose of his will.

Ephesians 1:11

When the night sky frays to day, smudged light coming up over fields,
I wake Levi.

Today's our date with the city hospital, an operating table, a
surgeon. He's sleepy. He drags to the back door, holding his splint and
bandaged hand to his chest, and I tie his shoelaces. The Farmer leans
against the open door and takes my hand and I take Levi's other one.
We will pray for the going, the cutting, the healing. Then it comes,
this murmur, and from my lips ...

"Lord ..." All the feelings since the blade and the breaking, all my
questioning and asking, they swell, hot lava to the surface, and I choke
it back, the thick farming hand squeezing mine.

" ... that I'd day after day after day greedily take what looks like
it's good from Your hand—a child gloating over sweet candy ..." My
voice catches hard. I've been a thief, trying to hoard away all the good.

" ... but that I'd thrash wild to escape when what You give from

Your hand feels bad—like gravel in the mouth. Oh, Father, *forgive* . . . Shall I accept good from You, and not trouble?"

I pray Job's words and heat flows down liquid.

What if that which feels like trouble, gravel in the mouth, is only that—*feeling*? What if faith says *all is* . . . I think it. But do I really mean it?

I gather up Levi and hand and the man at the door kisses us both good-bye and we wind through the dawn dark. The radio snaps out sound bites of presidents, celebrities. I click off the radio and flip over to Scripture on CD. The gospel of Matthew. In the slumber of towns, the odd kitchen light flashes by. *"Jesus said . . ."* *"And then Jesus replied . . ."* *"And a voice from heaven said . . ."* My fingers wrap hard around the steering wheel. At a graying intersection of two empty country roads, I idle long, stunned. It's coming out of the same stereo speakers, like the voices of presidents, dignitaries.

These are the words of God.

Headlights make holes in the slate morning. I nudge Levi gentle, awed, "We're listening to *God*." And out of the speakers I hear Him clear:

> But Jesus told him, "No! The Scriptures say,
>
> 'People do not live by bread alone,
> but by every word that comes from the mouth of God'"
> *Matthew 4:4 NLT*

I listen and I live. There is only *one* way to live full and it is "by every word that comes from the mouth of God."

It is all that Jesus used to survive in the desert, in His wrangle with silver-tongued Lucifer, only this: "It is written." And it's the Word of God that turns the rocks in the mouth to loaves on the tongue. That makes the eyes see, the body fill with light.

I glance at the clock. Levi is to roll into the operating theater in three hours. The Word of God whispers through the speakers. Levi drifts back to sleep. The countryside splits open, the earth unpeeled into sun. The wheat wears gold.

I drive out of dark and into morning glory, awakened to the strange truth that all new life comes out of the dark places, and hasn't it always been? Out of darkness, God spoke forth the teeming life. That wheat round and ripe across all these fields, they swelled as hope embryos in womb of the black earth. Out of the dark, tender life unfurled. Out of my own inner pitch, six human beings emerged, new life, wet and fresh.

All new life labors out of the very bowels of darkness.

Fullest life itself dawns from nothing but Calvary darkness and tomb-cave black into the radiance of Easter morning.

And there is no other way.

Then ... yes: It is suffering that has the realest possibility to bear down and deliver grace.

And grace that chooses to bear the cross of suffering overcomes that suffering.

I need to breathe.

I roll down the window. I inhale the pungency of a passing hayfield in bloom of clover, ditches with those all together wild black-eyed Susans swaying in early air. I try to think straight, truest straight. My pain, my dark—all the world's pain, all the world's dark—it might actually taste sweet to the tongue, be the genesis of new life?

Yes. And emptiness itself can birth the fullness of grace because in the emptiness we have the opportunity to turn to God, the only Begetter of grace, and there find all the fullness of joy.

So God transfigures all the world?

Darkness transfigures into light, bad transfigures into good, grief transfigures into grace, empty transfigures into full. God wastes nothing—makes everything work out according to His plan.

We pull into the hospital parking lot, and I park across from an entrance sign that reads Oncology. I open the door for Levi.

I wear my lenses and I pray to see. Who knows when you might climb a mount of transfiguration?

God, all the world is an opportunity to behold more of Your transfiguring darkness into grace. I won't ever get over it. I'm beholden to it all my life, now and forever. I want to accept all You give and learn to see into the darkness as You do, as a place to fill with Your light. Help me, Father. Help me to see in the dark.

strained grace

I will give thanks to the LORD because of his righteousness;
I will sing the praises of the name of the LORD Most High.

Psalm 7:17

This weekend there were guitars.

There were guitars and a hymn and there were voices rising and raised hands, and who could help it? "Were the whole realm of nature mine"—even this, the raised hands, the bowed head, the murmuring of thanks—it would be "an offering far too small."

I had thought this. I had thought this standing there worshiping with the guitars and strings. The empty space filling those guitars. The empty hands, released and raised. The cries all rising.

It can startle. In the willing hands of the believing, the emptiness can sing. He means to fill our emptiness with song. The way home, I had hummed quiet.

This weekend there were wounds. Sometime before bed, I say something offhand and he says nothing. He doesn't have to. I turn and can see it in his eyes and it's so loud. Hollowness can have a language of its own.

Behind a closed bedroom door he turns his back and I shake my head. Fling hands about, confused. Ugly. Want to raise my voice. I get the irony of this—and irony, it can hurt like swung steel. What I don't get is how he's not getting me and I'm not getting him and how did we get here so fast?

The empty space, it's between us. All this dark chamber.

It was after the guitars had been put in their cases that morning that someone had said it to me, told me about strings and space, about how to make music.

Music is made in stress. A string pulled tight, it has to be plucked, it has to be stressed. Moved from its comfortable, resting position. The bending of the string induces stress. As the string bends, as the string arches in stress and then releases, it vibrates—and there is the offering.

This one clear note, high and long. Stressed and empty and stretched right out, this is the space of song.

In stress there can be song. The resonance is in the surrender.

After the lights are turned out, I lie there in the dark, in this tight silence between us, remembering how the cries can rise.

Music could be here.

I ask and he speaks and I listen and try to echo back his heart, that I have heard him, and I turn to him, bend, move out of the comfortable position, out the rest of self-protection, and I reach for his hand. This bending, it's a stretch, a stress—but where else can the songs be found?

In the dark emptiness I find his and he squeezes my hand.

The resonance is always in the surrender.

The stress, the spaces right full of emptiness, these can be song makers. God means to make song out of stress. Out of all this emptiness.

Maybe this is always how to make life-worship: He holds tight and He strums and I could surrender to the music of God.

I shift a bit closer, and I'm retuned and returned, and it's there in the shadows, like a refrain—this sonorous offering of thanks.

Father God, I bend the knee knowing: You intend to take all my stress and make it song. I bend the knee knowing: the resonance of my life happens in surrender. I bend the knee and offer You my emptiness — in You it can sing.

re-membering grace

Jesus said, "Were not ten healed? Where are the nine?
Can none be found to come back and give glory to God except
this outsider?" Then he said to him, "Get up. On your way.
Your faith has healed and saved you."

Luke 17:18 MSG

A silly little turn of my foot in a game of charades gone ridiculously wrong.

And the bones in my ankle disengage, swell my foot like a bluing balloon, and I writhe quiet and smile thin.

Because really, aren't I one of those women who comes unglued and broken only a thousand times a day?

The heart of this world is fractured and we all bear the fault lines.

I ice my throbbing ankle hill with a Ziploc bag of melting snow.

Hobble around with the laundry for days.

I'm lying on the couch with my foot propped high over my head, when a friend e-mails, "Pray for me? I can manage the nausea and exhaustion. It's the mouth sores that are the hardest."

She's the mother of five young children.

"I'm just not sure how I'll be able to do my job to take care of my babies while on these drugs every day."

She's on an aggressive, determined round of three chemo drugs.

"I am just thankful that such a medicine exists and there continues to be things to do that keep me living and mothering."

She's a mother with stage-three invasive breast cancer. The universe's right shattered. My heart leaks through all the cracks. And she's thankful.

I limp over piles of books. Try to get away from everything shattered. Kids argue loud and doors slam and floors shake and I sigh weary. I pick up the peels of an orange left to wither on the coffee table, a whole sphere right skinned. On the way to the garbage can, I stumble, stub my good foot on the rocking chair. I howl. Flail. Dance hobble back to the kitchen.

And I pray for the sores oozing in a mouth of a mama singing lullabies to her babies. This is one busted-up, hurting world and I want all the mothers to live. *You hear me, God? Live!*

Why can't this woman, whom I love, breathe for years more and hold her babies till they grow old and laugh at the wonder of eighteenth birthdays and lie there in the dark listening to their heavy slumber, all their lungs and life rising and filling and falling, rhythms of grace?

Why can't she grow old enough to pluck out a few gray hairs, live long enough to have hands wrinkled with memories and real love, to stand with her husband and wonder over grandbabies?

Why do I sit across the table from her and listen to her say the words — that the doctors don't expect her to see spring. *Oh God, please hear our cries!*

And the planet spins with a mother who isn't bitter but gives thanks to God for the medicine that takes her hair and her strength but keeps her living and mothering one day more, that keeps her over the sink with a cloth and over the toilet with a brush and over their pillows with prayers just one day more ...

And if she can be thankful for the chemo killing her cells to keep her alive just for today with no guarantees for tomorrow — can't I sing the lullaby of gratitude to my own moaning soul? Just for today?

And I am just thankful, Lord, for . . .

But can I remember? What am I thankful for? My foot's killing me. And it's not killing me at all.

And that's just the point . . .

This fallen world never stops dis-membering who we are. We're all breaking a bit more every day, even in small ways. And there, even as we ache, is the gentle whisper of God. With the quiet urging to give thanks anyways, to do this in re-membrance of Him. But why in the world give thanks? Why in the name of heaven?

Because when we remember how He blesses, loves us, when we recollect His goodnesses to us, we heal — we re-member.

In the remembering to give thanks, our broken places are re-membered — made whole.

When we re-member all His blessings, we re-member all our fractures, and in giving thanks in the assembly it's our very souls that re-assemble.

Is that it? That the mama with cancer giving thanks for right now — she is the one who is fully really living? *All in Him, all giving glory.*

At the table I prop up my swollen foot and murmur thanks to Him — for a chair, for a leg, me hobbling through mothering today, giving thanks to Him who let Himself be broken to make us whole, and doing this thanks in remembrance of His daily grace, it re-members and mends me and the pain eases.

The fracture lines in my heart all healing in this fusion to Him.

~

Lord, today, in the broken places, cause me to give thanks, to do what You ask, in re-membrance of You. So I may recollect all Your goodnesses, so I may heal — and re-member.

storm grace

Therefore, since we are receiving a kingdom that cannot be shaken,
let us be thankful, and so worship God acceptably
with reverence and awe.

Hebrew 12:28

"If God really works in everything, then why don't we thank Him for everything?"

She asks me this straight out.

My daughter, Hope, and I, we sit in the truck on the field's hem, waiting to give the Farmer his lunch.

The Farmer is planting bean seeds into earth's dark bed. The sky is rising darker in the west.

He races rain.

"For every drop of rain You keep from falling on us as we plant— thank You, Lord ..."

I had murmured the prayer, water splatting hard against the windshield of the pickup.

We need at least one more day of dry weather to plant a year's worth of beans, our livelihood.

"And for every drop of rain that You do let fall—thank You, Lord ..." My daughter, Hope, whispers her strange echo.

Really? I turn, searching her face.

She looks me right in the eye.

"If God really works in everything, then why don't we thank Him for everything? Why do we accept good from His hand—and not bad?"

This is hard. Maybe the hardest of all. She is young. She has much to come.

I have held dying babies. Eaten with those who live in the town garbage heap. Wept with women who've been violated, with the bankrupt, the heart-crushed, the terminal. And this never stops being true: Neglecting to give thanks only deepens the wound of the world.

Doesn't God call His people to a nondiscriminating response in all circumstances? "Giving thanks always and for everything" (Ephesians 5:20 ESV).

If I only thank Him when the fig tree buds—is this "selective faith"? Practical atheism? What of faith in a God who wastes nothing? Who makes all into grace?

And yet, is thanking God for everything ... thanking Him for evil?

Rivulets run down glass, blurring my husband and all our seeded prayers. What do I accurately see and know?

When we bought the Enemy's lie in the beginning and ate from the Tree of the Knowledge of Good and Evil, Satan hissed then that we'd really see and know what is good and evil.

But the Father of Lies, he'd duped us in the whole nine yards. Though we ate of that tree, we did not become like God.

We have no knowledge of good and evil apart from God. My seeing, it is not omniscient. Can I really see if a death, disaster, dilemma, is actually evil? Mine is only to faithfully see His Word and wholly obey Him in this. Therein is the Tree of Life.

Is this why He commands us to give thanks *always and for everything*? Because to thank God in all is to refuse Satan's relentless lure to be godlike in all.

To thank God in all is to bend the knee in allegiance to God, who alone knows all.

To thank God in all is to give God glory in all. Is this not our chief end?

When I only give thanks for some things, aren't I likely to miss giving God glory in most things?

Murmuring thanks doesn't deny that an event is a tragedy and neither does it deny that there's a cracking fissure straight across the heart.

Giving thanks is only this: making the canyon of pain into a megaphone to proclaim the ultimate goodness of God.

Our thanks to God is our witness to the goodness of God when Satan and all the world would sneer at us to recant.

I lay my hand on the rain-filmed windowpane and I see clearer. But this is not easy: That which I refuse to thank Christ for, I refuse to believe Christ can redeem.

The gray sky is drumming steady on the truck's tin roof.

His perfect love casts out all fears and leaves only thanks and I listen to her sing it, like a chorus with the rain: Thank You, Lord. Thank You, Lord.

Like a song from the belly of the fish, like a Jonah refrain echoing off the walls of the great fish: "But I with the voice of thanksgiving will sacrifice to you ..." (Jonah 2:9 ESV)

Like a haunting, holy answer to what she asks, the song of the saints, always thanksgiving—practicing here the only song that will be sung at the very last of time: "Praise and glory and wisdom and thanks ... be to our God for ever and ever" (Revelation 7:12 ESV).

Thank You, Lord. I lilt it soft with her, faith's brazen song facing storms ...

The rain falling hard now.

Lord God, I thank You in all things, to refuse Satan's relentless lure to be godlike in all things. I bend my knee in allegiance to You, who alone knows all. I praise You in all, to give You glory in all and make my canyon of pain into a megaphone to proclaim Your ultimate goodness. There is nothing I refuse to thank You for—because I am convinced there is nothing You won't redeem.

breathing grace

... in his grace there is life;
weeping may be for a night,
but joy comes in the morning.
Psalm 30:5 BBE

The ring Sara sent me in June, it didn't fit my middle finger.

She'd worn it on her middle finger—until its sterling silver weight had made her enflamed knuckles burn.

That's when she wound it off slow, slipped it in an envelope, and had it dropped off at the post office.

Because she knew—the fire in my bones had been about extinguished.

And if I wore it, would I feel the heat ignite?

The letter she'd tucked in with the ring read:

I am sending you my favorite silver ring I used to wear on my middle finger every day. I can't wear it anymore as it's too heavy on my sore fingers . . . It is purposefully hammered and bent, the way I often felt—the way you are feeling—but it is beautiful and perfect in its imperfections.

I don't know how Sara knew this season had battered hard. Don't know when I told her that fear sometimes made my teeth chatter. How to keep breathing when your bones feel a bit deadened and ash-gray?

I wrote to her one night, my first real letter to her:

I wish you were here tonight, Sara. The sun is setting over the snow all melting. The world is pink and glowing, warm and resting. The dishwasher is twirling, swirling, humming. Shalom is here in the rocking chair reading aloud to herself from her reader . . . little whispers . . . sounding words out.

I wanted to share the beauty of this moment with you, Sara. Just to sit with you and share eucharisteo with you. And when I see things that make me sing and ache and give thanks for the wonder of this amazing grace, just this moment, I think of how you live what I long to.

Sara had turned all the pages in that story of *eucharisteo* that I had stumbled to scratch awkwardly down.

Her very first letter to me had said her vocabulary had a new word: *eucharisteo*. She wasn't simply reading it; she was living it. She wrote it on her wall, painted it on canvas, pinned to her inspiration board. Her spine was fusing and her lungs ached and she smiled a bit weakly to think she might live decades with an eight on the pain scale, housebound three years because this world's air would kill her — but she was taking every moment as grace, *charis*, giving thanks for it, and finding joy, *chara*. Grace, gratitude, joy — *eucharisteo*.

Sara chose joy.

And I told her I carried her with me wherever I went — on planes, across the mountains, out to the ocean, right to the edge. Me, the woman terrified to leave her house, wearing the ring of the woman who couldn't leave hers.

When I didn't think I could walk out the door and keep breathing, I'd feel the ring. Sara would stand at the door and dance if she had this chance. I couldn't contort this blessing into a burden.

She had told me once, "I had to choose fear — or completely trust Him. One cannot exist if the other is true."

So I walked out my door and I breathed. Stepping into fears can be the first step into real faith and focusing the eyes on all the grace here keeps the focus on His all-sufficient grace.

Fear is banished in this present moment when the presence of I AM fills it. We could do that: Practice the awareness of God's filling present. Sara had written it too:

> *The pain is present and I know I'm getting slower, but this is it: to live for this moment and this moment only. I'm just thankful He's with me. That I'm never lonely for Him.*
>
> *And my gift today? There is a tree in front of another building that I can see from my window. There was a slow breeze today, and the branches drifted back and forth so slowly, like they were dancing and waving to me.*
>
> *I had to resist the urge to wave back.*

Sara chose joy and saw grace and she waved back.

I sent her photos of the flowers on the front porch, practicing the praise of God in the present, sent photos of smiling friends who choose joy with her.

And in a few weeks Sara smiles back from the screen's webcam and tells me in this gravelly voice, coughing it out, that she is saying it too: *Yes* to God. I have to turn from the screen, everything running liquid. She says it too? She knows it too: When we need peace, we only need to say yes to God's purposes.

How can she say that? Because she lives what she believes—and she scrawls it everywhere and all over my heart: eucharisteo. *Yes, God, yes!*

Grace, gratitude, joy—*eucharisteo.*

And a night in late September, after hospice is called in and she knows she's finally, thankfully, turned homeward, Sara writes:

> *I don't think I'll be able to write again as I'm getting too weak, but you need to know—when you feel weak, take a deep breath.*

I close my eyes tight, blink it all back. Sara knows what biblical scholars know, the very name of God—*YHWH*—sounds like our breathing—aspirated consonants. God Himself names Himself—and the name He chooses is the sound of our own breathing.

When you are weak, take a deep breath. That's what Sara said at the end: Breathe. Say His name. Say yes to God. *Eucharisteo.*

Her last words to me, they blink up in an e-mail: "You will never be alone or need to be afraid."

I reach out to touch the screen, touch her one last time, ring touching her last pixels and she is still breathing.

As long as she breathes, she says yes to God.

I keep my hands there on the screen, on Sara's words, on Sara—her encircling me in silver, my bones all burning love and Him and joy.

And my daughter, Hope, she's playing it in the night shadows again, playing it again tonight, "Cherry Blossoms in Rain" on the piano, the song she now calls "Sara's Song"—her fingers, all her fingers, playing the notes.

And again there's an ache, a haunting echo, and the notes like the Oriental East, like a winging or a long leaving, like standing at the edge of what once was and witnessing the losing of something pure and prayed for.

After the last high note, Hope whispers it into the stilled dark: "Mama? That whole song, it's played on the black notes."

The black notes. The black notes make music too.

Somewhere in the house, in the dark, I can hear it—how a door opens, how Sara now walks straight through into light.

When she turns and waves back to grace, I'll take a deep breath and wave to the extraordinary joy of her too, her silver ring shimmering on my hand here ...

The weight of all His sheer glory.

Lord God, my every breath is saying Your name. Even when my life seems to be playing only black notes — how can I not choose eucharisteo: grace, gratitude, joy?

amaryllis grace

"Surely, just as I have intended so it has happened,
and just as I have planned so it will stand."
Isaiah 14:24 NASB

Why in the world, everywhere I turn, every page, always death? I'd like some happy, blithe, Pollyanna words, please. For a happy, blithe, Pollyanna life.

My gratitude journal lies open on the counter. I retrieve it, flip back through pages, and run my hand over penned numbers, memories of the Pollyanna moments. And I can see it in the looking back, how this daily practice of the discipline of gratitude is the way to daily practice the delight of God and what in the spring had been #362 *suds in the sink* grew over weeks and months.

G. K. Chesterton had said it, "Joy is the gigantic secret of the Christian."[36] This counting blessings, it's the unlocking of the mystery of joy, joy hiding in gratitude. Aren't the Jesus people the most thankful?

And then it had seemed like it might be over all too soon. Come early winter, I jotted haltingly, not wanting it to end. And when I wrote the one thousandth gift, I had written careful:

1000. Resurrection bloom, an amaryllis

My mother-in-law had given us that amaryllis bulb the year before.

182

I had set it in the kitchen windowsill, under the porcelain dove. I had waited. A full rotation of the earth through the galaxy, I had waited. Cancer had left Mom Voskamp's remains buried deep. And then. Her bulb had trumpeted a call: *Fully live! Live fully!* My one thousandth gift. I had swallowed hard. God had used the dare to give me this; led me all the way to give me this as the thousandth gift, exactly like this, to unfurl just this: *Live fully!* Mom Voskamp spoke to me from the grave. Here are gifts worth waiting 365 days for, gifts worth counting to one thousand for, gifts that will unbelievably emerge out of the deathly dark. Joy is always worth the wait, and fully living always worth the believing. The pursuit! The bloom had trumpeted for weeks.

I had read it in Job, what makes reading God's message in every moment a form of art, a masterpiece of the fullest life: God speaks to us not in one language but two: "For God does speak — now one way, now another" (33:14). One way, His finger writing words in stars (Psalm 19:1 – 3), His eternal power written naked in all creation (Romans 1:20); and now another way, the sharp Holy Writ of Scripture that makes a careful incision into a life, blade words that kindly cut the tissue back to where soul and spirit join, tenderly laying bare the intents of the heart (Hebrews 4:12).

To read His message in all the moments, in the waiting moments, the dark moments, the moments before the blooming, I'll need to read His passion on the page; wear the lens of the Word, to read His writing in the world. Only the Word is the answer to rightly reading the world.

I had kept turning the pages. And into another year, another spring, another year of beans and corn and wheat under sun, I had kept writing it down, a free-for-all, a journal in my purse, one by my bed, another on the counter by the sink, a file on my computer, because the dare to write *one thousand* gifts becomes the dare to celebrate innumerable, *endless* gifts! That initial discipline, the daily game to count, keep counting to one thousand, it was God's necessary tool to reshape me, remake me, rename me—unfurl me.

Daily discipline is the door to full freedom and the discipline to count to one thousand gave way to the freedom of wonder and I can't imagine not staying awake to God in the moment, the joy in the now.

Was this now only the beginning of really becoming?

God, all that You make is good. And all that seems to oppose Your will is but a tool to accomplish it. Change my perspective today to see beyond the shadows, above the clouds, where the light never stops shining. Plant the truth of it in me: there are gifts worth counting to one thousand for, gifts that will emerge out of the deathly dark. Unfurl amaryllis grace today through the daily discipline of counting gifts, for I believe it: Joy is always worth the wait!

happiest grace

For the sin of this one man, Adam, brought death to many.
But even greater is God's wonderful grace and his gift of forgiveness
to many through this other man, Jesus Christ.
Romans 5:15 NLT

During the hour drive it takes to get to the lake on a Sunday afternoon, I think of that sermon we'd had in the morning. The preacher preaching pure gospel, how to be born again.

Twenty-five years he's been preaching it in our little country chapel, to the hog farmers, the corn croppers, the mothers with babies in arms. How you can't work for God's love, angle for it, or jockey for it—you can't earn God's love. *You can only turn toward God's love.*

When we all unpile at the lake, the little girls run and cousins squeal happy at the water's edge.

My mama and I, we stand there, toes in sand and the wind blowing back hair ...

Our faces turned right toward the sun.

It's a gift, the preacher said. Salvation *is* the gift, the one wrapped in God taking on skin, laying His bare love out for the world, arms spreading to the very ends of the limbs of the tree of life.

There is their laughter. There is their running. There is my mama smiling. There is that singular seagull writing across the sky. These are gifts. They beg praise to Him. Holy joy lies in the habit of murmuring thanks to God for the smallest of graces. I falter, but this is the habit to wear for a lifetime.

And really? There is only one gift—the one ocean of Christ that falls as rain over us in a thousand ways.

Christ is the offering and salvation is the gift and repentance is what makes us recipients of grace. *Christ* is the gift. *Christ* is the bridge home. *Christ* is our joy. How can I forget this, ever stop giving thanks for Him alone?

Happiness is not getting something but being given to Someone.

It is the sacrifice of Christ that returns us to God and communion with Him is possible anywhere and bless the Lord, oh, my soul, bless the very Maker of my soul.

Water keeps washing up over my toes.

A whole sea rushing up to meet the feet turned.

A sea rushing up to the shore and washing the feet turned . . .

And a Father catching his girl falling . . . all this happiness . . . just in Him, right until last light.

Oh God, my God, holy joy lies in the habit of murmuring thanks to You for the smallest of graces. Forgive my faltering and make this thanksgiving to You the habit I'll wear all of my life. Because You, my Lord and Savior, You are the one Gift, the one Bridge—the one Ocean that falls as rain over me in a thousand ways. Kindle my heart again, to know that happiness is not getting something but being given to Someone.

comforting grace

Shout for joy, you heavens;
rejoice, you earth;
burst into song, you mountains!
For the LORD comforts his people
and will have compassion on his afflicted ones.

Isaiah 49:13

I hear it on Sunday, thinking our preacher's looking straight at me, me trying to look away:

When God moves us out of our comfort zone—into places that are way bigger than us, places that are difficult, hard, painful, places that even hurt—*this is a gift.*

We are being given a gift.

These hard places give us the gift of intimately knowing God in ways that would never be possible in our comfort zones.

Where's the back door of the chapel? *I'd like out.*

I look out the window to snow coming down. Shift hard in my chair. Can't find any comfortable position. I've been way out of my comfort zone for months. God taking this book I'd written, my story with my bare heart, taking me way out of my comfort zone.

All the way to the Bible Study Sisters on Saturday morning, I'd told myself I wasn't opening my mouth, not saying a word, not letting anyone into how all this felt. And when the other Anne had looked up from Zechariah 8 and asked me how it was for me, I didn't say a thing, couldn't, for everything quavering, heart running all liquid. I had mouthed it to the ceiling, a murmur looking up, trying to keep it all from spilling. "How did I get here?"

When God moves us out of our comfort zone . . . When God . . .

We're in the God-zone when we're out of our comfort zone and the Holy Spirit, our Comforter, comforts us when we step outside our comfort zone. It's only in the uncomfortable places that we can experience the tenderness of the Comforter.

When everything opened and fell on Saturday morning, Annette had left her chair to come and hold me and Mama had reached over and squeezed my hand and I had brushed it back, smiled, believing. Knowing. Anne had prayed long and earnest and I had felt the Spirit's embrace, like the warmth of the sun laying its arm down across my shoulder. I had felt it, how the sun had shone.

We're in step with the Holy Spirit when we step out into hard things. Faith gets out of the boat. And walking in the Spirit means stepping out to walk in the waves and feeling the comfort of His grip. *Isn't this gift?*

And on Sunday morning I look across the sanctuary. Can you really say that to the girl who doesn't wear her engagement ring anymore, to the beautiful mother whose husband left and the cancer has come, to the bent widow sitting next to the empty chair? Can you really say that to them, to the world? That the greatest gift we can ever receive is the gift of losing our earthly security and comfort? So that we can unwrap the intimacy of the Savior and His heavenly comfort.

I swallow hard.

Counting one thousand gifts is about *eucharisteo*, that Greek word that expresses what Christ did at the Last Supper: take the bread of pain as grace. Give thanks for that which is hard. Endure the cross, all in view of the joy set before.

Counting one thousand gifts means counting the hard things— *otherwise I've miscounted.*

After Sunday lunch and the dishes, I sit with the kids opening up a game board and I open a book and read this: "Ecstasy comes from the Greek word *ekstasis. Ek* meaning out. And *stasis* meaning standstill. Ecstatic = out of static."

I close the book. He keeps whispering it to my trembling heart, to me who knows and then forgets: Those who fully live, who live ecstatic lives of joy, embrace moving out of comfort zones. Ecstatic joy is found outside of static comfort zones. Because it's moving out to where the Spirit moves. The Spirit is never static. Never standstill. Like the wind, the Spirit always moves.

Shalom crawls up onto my lap. I lay the book down but I hold on to the words.

"Mrs. Nagel told me at church that she'd seen flowers poking up before this snow came. Do you think they are still out there somewhere, underneath the snow, Mama?" She looks out the window.

The snow's still coming down, a mystery of white.

"There are signs of spring out there." I tuck a curl behind her ear and say it soft. "Outside, in the cold, still signs of spring. Gifts coming."

She smiles, rubs her hands happy.

Outside of comfort's warmth, gifts unfurling underneath. Signs of radical change emerging everywhere.

Winter being overturned, of *eucharisteo* in the midst of hard things —of a revolution of thanks in all things to the God over all things.

Shalom and I fill a pitcher of water for the crocuses on the table. She counts the blooms. "There are seven!"

I smile at her so ecstatic.

And I stand there watching ...

Watching the water flow out into this ponding circle and then moving out, always farther and further out.

Lord, thank You for the gift of coaxing me out of my comfort zone and further into the comfort of You. I really trust You enough to say it today: Thank You for the gift of losing my earthly security and comfort—so that I can unwrap the intimacy of You and Your heavenly comfort. Today, Father God, move me out of static comfort zones so I may know the ecstatic joy of the comfort of Christ!

cycling grace

"Holy, holy, holy is the LORD Almighty;
the whole earth is full of his glory."

Isaiah 6:3

In an endless cycle of grace He gives us gifts to serve the world. This is how to make a life great and *eucharisteo* embarks us on the path: "Whoever wants to become great among you must be your servant, and whoever wants to be first must be your slave" (Matthew 20:26–27).

Outside my window, the whole of creation chooses just this. The leaves of the maple tree freely unfurl oxygen, clouds overhead grow pregnant with rain to bless, the soil of our fields offer up yield. All His created world throbs with the joy in *eucharisteo*: "It is more blessed to give than to receive" (Acts 20:35).

This is the way Jesus Himself chose. "That is what the Son of Man has done: He came to serve, not be served—and then to give away his life in exchange for the many who are held hostage" (Matthew 20:28 MSG).

It's the astonishing truth that while I serve Christ, it is He who serves me. Jesus Christ still lives with a towel around His waist, bent in service to His people ... in service to me as I serve, that I need never serve in my own strength. Jesus Christ, who came into this world "not to be served but to serve, and to give his life as a ransom for many" (Mark 10:45), will one day come again and "put on an apron, and serve them as they sit and eat!" (Luke 12:37 NLT), and even this very day He faithfully serves that we might say, "The Lord is my helper" (Hebrews 13:6).

Every day for a month we as a family read together Isaiah 58, and we can't get over it and we come to know it in the marrow and the fiber:

> Feed the hungry,
>   and help those in trouble.
> Then your light will shine out from the darkness,
>   and the darkness around you will be as bright as noon.
> The LORD will guide you continually,
>   giving you water when you are dry
>   and restoring your strength.
> You will be like a well-watered garden,
>   like an ever-flowing spring.
>
> *Isaiah 58:10– 11 NLT*

It's the fundamental, lavish, radical nature of the upside-down economy of God.

Empty to fill.

While the Deceiver jockeys to dupe us into thinking otherwise, we who are made in the image of God, being formed into Christ's likeness, our happiness comes too, not in the having, but in the handing over. Give your life away in exchange for many lives, give away your blessings to multiply blessings, give away so that many might increase—and do it all for the love of God. I can bless, pour out, be broken and given in our home and the larger world and never fear that there won't be enough to give.

Eucharisteo has taught me to trust that there is always enough God.

He has no end. He calls us to serve, and it is Him whom we serve, but He, very God, kneels down to serve us as we serve. The servant-hearted never serve alone. Spend the whole of your one wild and beautiful life investing in many lives, and God simply will not be outdone.

God extravagantly pays back everything we give away and exactly in the currency that is not of this world but of the one we yearn for: *joy in Him.*

Father God, the glorious God from whom and through whom and to whom are all things, You reign and You rain down blessings, that my life may become a blessing. Lord God, please—pour me out in this place, my life used up in Your endless cycle of grace.

wearing grace

The LORD your God is in your midst,
a mighty one who will save;
he will rejoice over you with gladness;
he will quiet you by his love;
he will exult over you with loud singing.

Zephaniah 3:17 ESV

It'd been a bit of an everyday miracle — us leaving the farm and all those baby pigs out in the barn and traveling to Ecuador to meet children sponsored through the Christian humanitarian organization, Compassion International.

On our first day in Ecuador, on a steep mountainside under direct sun, we bent beside Rosa, a pig farmer herself, and planted potatoes into her loamy earth.

Rosa's youngest, little Liliana, she scooped up a puppy right there next to the potato patch and she just hid behind its gaping mouth, her eyes all large and laughing.

Rosa told us what Liliana had done — that Liliana had found that puppy wandering abandoned, lost, outside her classroom. That Liliana had brought the puppy home to love. That Liliana loved. And when Liliana gaped all happy, just like the puppy, I laughed right out loud.

And there it was again, words from *One Thousand Gifts*—and I could feel it again, the joy of it welling: *We receive grace.*

And through us, grace could flow on. Like a cycle of water in continuous movement, grace is meant to fall, a rain ... again, again, again. We could share the grace, multiply the joy, extend the table of the feast, enlarge the paradise of His presence.

We are blessed. We can bless. This is happiness.

We are blessed, and couldn't we bless and couldn't this fullness flow on and on and on and isn't this the realest happiness?

Liliana, living in a single-parent home, living in abject poverty, looking for a sponsorship through Compassion, Liliana with less than little, she brings a puppy home just to love, and I'm the one scooping it up, what really is—that the giving away is the getting of joy.

After a week of beautiful children and praying with families up the Amazon and serving with pastors planting churches, we fly a continent home. And a week later, and a whole half a world north of Liliana and her puppy, I wake up strangely happy. Life change is as simple as changing our choices, and transformation is fully possible when we form our decisions differently—form them into the image of Christ.

A fashion catalog comes in the mail. Models standing beside llamas in the village of some cobbled South American street. I've just seen it, the dirt floors, the dark and no sinks, behind the doors on the street where the model sways thin in her $588 dress. I think of Rosa's one bran-sack window and how she turned away when her heart rained grief. Poverty can't be airbrushed and it hides its tears and you won't see it modeled on the front covers of glossy magazines.

I like the model's shoes.

How in the world can I like her shoes?

There is this, and it unknots everything in me, smoothes me out, and it's the way the choices change: *What if we wanted to be beautiful more than we wanted to buy beautiful?*

The Enemy tempts that stuff is what makes us lovely—when the Truth is surrender makes us the loveliest and what is more lovely than love? Love, it knows no other way than to give away.

Liliana, she had mimicked puppy joy and I had laughed right out loud and so had she, and the moment, it had light all along the seams. What could be lovelier than this? Her loving a lost puppy and me loving her and Christ loving all the lost? Why not change all the choices for this? Model all that matters, the Beautiful, a life like Christ's—and imitate Christ's joy—the way He gives.

The way the happiness and healing is always in the opening of a hand, the opening a life to the largeness of God. It stays with me and I wear *this*, the joy of it—the way Liliana laughed in all her sheer loveliness.

Lord of my life, what if I wanted to be beautiful more than I wanted to buy beautiful? Though the Enemy tempts that stuff is what makes me lovely, remind me that surrender to You makes us the loveliest and what is more lovely than counting the ways You love? Change my life by changing my choices and transform me by forming my decisions into the image of the sheer loveliness of Christ.

trumpeting grace

Let the heart of those who seek the LORD be glad …
Seek His face continually.
Remember His wonderful deeds which he has done.

1 Chronicles 16:10–12 NASB

I hadn't agreed with everything in the book I'd picked up, but right after I read that one story, I went looking for an old horn to screw right to the wall—because there really are things worth the proclaiming.

And when I find this one old horn, I walk around the house, horn in hand, trying to figure if it looks best on this wall?

Or maybe on the back of this door? The Farmer raises his eyebrows.

"A horn on a wall?" He's grinning boyish. Joshua is playing scales. Levi's reciting Latin chants. Shalom and Malakai are arguing loud over a game of chess.

"Because you're thinking it's not quite loud enough in here yet?"

"You!" I poke him in the shoulder, him broad like a beam that carries half my world. "Does it look right here?"

"I think I've got a wall out in the barn it might look perfect on." He winks, shields himself with his arm to fend off the next poke.

"But if you knew the story …" I try to defend and he nods,

knowing, smiling, "Uh-huh." And I nod, knowing stories can turn around whole hard hearts. Jesus walked back roads and spun stories and turned around lives and the axis of the cosmos.

So I tell this story at lunch.

"A man drove a stretch of highway past this tattered cardboard sign that read 'Honk if you're happy.'" I pass down the squash.

And who doesn't roll his eyes at such naïveté? As if the world is this strange hybrid of Pollyanna and Sesame Street—if you're happy and you know it, *honk, honk*—when it's really just a strange new, old world, broken and a mess. Shalom offers me her glass and I pour water.

"But there's this one day when the man drives past the sign with his little girl, and on a whim he beeps the horn. And every day when he passes the sign, his daughter begs him to do it again, and pretty soon, every time he's on this stretch of highway, this jaded man, this cynical man, is anticipating the sign. Anticipating honking his horn. And do you know what he said?"

I want to make sure I get it right. I push back my chair, to get the library book from my nightstand. Flip through the pages ... There—that one good story in the book:

> Deep inside and just for a moment, I felt a little happier than I had just seconds before—as if honking the horn made me happier ... If on a one-to-ten scale, I was feeling an emotional two, when I honked the horn, my happiness grew several points ...
>
> In time, when I turned on to Highway 544, I noticed that my emotional setpoint would begin to rise. That entire 13.4 mile stretch began to become a place of emotional rejuvenation for me.[37]

I lay the book down on the table, reach for the water pitcher.

"See what happened to him? The sign read, 'Honk if you're happy.' And he discovered that the act of honking the horn—it made him happy."

"Honk, honk!" Malakai grins at the end of the table. His mouth's full of food. I love him wild.

"So who puts up a cardboard sign beside a highway—Honk if you're happy?" I have to get to the rest of the story before the table erupts into a fest of honking Canadians.

"This man has to find out. So he finds a house on the other side of the trees that line the highway—and he goes up to the door and asks the folks if they know anything about the happy sign. And the man at the door welcomes him in and says yes, yes, he made the sign."

And this is why he made the sign: Because he was sitting there every day in his house, sitting there in a darkened bedroom with his young wife who was terminal, sitting there watching her every day as she lay there waiting to die. And one day when he really couldn't take it anymore, he painted up that sign and stuck it out by the road. Because, he said—I reach for the book again, to find the right page, to get the words right: "I just wanted people in their cars not to take this moment for granted. This special, never-again-to-be-repeated moment with the ones they care for most should be savored and they should be aware of the happiness in the moment."[38]

I look around at all their faces ringing the table, the jewel of them slipping around me in this space. Light's falling across the table. Hope's one strand of loose hair is its own gold. Something inside me trumpets loud and long.

I can only whisper the end of the story.

At first, after the man had put out the sign, there was only a honk here and there, and his dying wife asked what that was about and the husband explained how he'd put the sign out there and after a few days there was more and more honking. And the husband said that the honking . . .

I look down again at the book but everything's blurring. Finally the line surfaces.

... became like medicine to her. As she lay there, she heard the horns and found great comfort in knowing that she was not isolated in a dark room dying. She was part of the happiness of the world. It was literally all around her.[39]

It was literally all around her.
So much light's falling across the table.
"I'm thinking it will look best in that doorway."
The Farmer winks.
And when the Farmer heads out to the shop after lunch, I call after him — *Remember to bring in a screwdriver so we can hang the horn!*
And he waves back to me as he runs across the farmyard. And when I'm standing in the kitchen wiping off the counters, I hear it clear, from the farm pickup parked out in the laneway, out by the shop: Honk! Honk! Honk!
I laugh. He's out there honking the horn of his truck!
I turn to the window, laughing ... He's happy! *Happy* ...
And I reach for my pen atop my open gratitude journal there on the counter. "Honk if you're happy" is really "to be happy, honk."
And "give thanks if you are joy-filled" is really "to be joy-filled, *give thanks.*"
And I write it down. "The Farmer honking a horn — and that grin of his."
This has become like medicine to me.
Shalom waves to the Farmer from the window. He's waving back at her. She sings the words quiet to him, "Honk if you're happy!" — and she knows he can't hear.
But all the world is heaven's clarion and even in the dark, we are surrounded by it, all the happiness of the world, and I keep the journal close, the thanks ready.
Because literally — it was all around her.

Thank You, God, for the horns You place in my life every day—the chances to honk and be happy. Show me more! And if a joy-filled heart is good medicine, then giving thanks is my daily prescription. Lord, You make all this world heaven's clarion and even in the dark I am surrounded by it and let me do it a thousand times today—offer honking thanks up to Your throne—joy ringing through all the earth and me!

becoming grace

I will bless you ... and you will be a blessing.
Genesis 12:2

I walk in our back door to candlelight still flickering, hang the keys on the hook, and look around at the steep mountain of laundry there in the mudroom, the shoes scattered, a coat dropped. The mudroom sink is grime ringed. Fingerprints smear across the mirror.

I laugh the happiest wonder.

In the afternoon's drizzle, I give happy thanks for the daily mess with a smile a mile wide because this is again my chance to wholeheartedly serve God, to do full-bodied *eucharisteo* with the hands and the heart and the lips. I can count each task a gift, pure *eucharisteo*.

Grace!

This work—the thousand endless jobs—they each give the opportunity for one to *become* the gift, *a thousand times over!* Because with every one of the thousand endless jobs, I become the gift to God and to others because this work is the public God serving, the daily liturgy of thanks, the completing of the Communion service with my service.

Eucharisteo wakens me wide-eyed and nodding to the truth that I—a mother of six—now *own* a truth bought with the practice of *eucharisteo*.

I reach out and touch the reflection in the splattered mirror over the sink and whisper into those eyes: Yes, today, *again*, yes, *you can bless!* Here you can enact *eucharisteo*; here you can become a current in a river of grace that redeems the world.

Even me. I think of my brother-in-law, John. John, who had buried his two sons, who let me into his healing through crazy grief when he said, "The way through the pain is to reach out to others in theirs." I have known ache and becoming the blessing is what deeply blesses us and this is the way He binds up our wounds.

I think back to earlier, washing each other's feet at the women's small group. How we take Communion. Then, quietly, I fill the basins with water warm and circled together as a community we *give* communion. We bare our toes, soles, and I bend with sisters in Christ, dip my hands into water, and touch shy skin. We wash feet, all around, we wash feet. We lap water across skin and I hold a woman's heel and I gently bathe and as group facilitator I ask each in the room to think about this washing of feet as symbolic of our lives on a grand scale, of how we are called to complete the Communion service in service. I tilt my head to look into her face and I ask it quiet in a quiet room: "Do you, in your day-to-day life, feel served? How might we as a community better serve you?"

And she, mother of eight, an elder's wife, children's ministry leader, one who pours her life out in unending ways, she whispers, haltingly through emotion. "But I'm the one who needs to ask if I've been a blessing."

"But you— *oh, how you have blessed.*" With the tepid water, I wash her toes, these beads between fingers, and I recount the long string of ways she's intimately blessed me: "The day you took me for a walk through the woods and listened to the faint heartbeat of my faith. The countless words you have sent me, a hand of friendship." I take the cloth and wash her heel. "The way you have been real with me, transparent and authentic, and we have been mothers and we have been sisters and we have wept." And I look up into her face, her wet feet in my hands, and again the chin wobbles all feeling. In this room of women, washing feet, it overflows. With memories of the ways each has become the blessing. Unmasked, we wash our faces in tears of joy. Hands cupping dripping soles, I see how it is our very presence in each other's lives that makes us the gift. By the very function not of our doing *but of our being*, I see we are the beloved of God.

And so we *become* the love of God, blessing those He loves.

And even here, right where I am, I can become the blessing again, a little life that multiplies joy, making the larger world a better place.

God can enter into me, even me, and use these hands, these feet, to be His love, a love that goes on and on and on forever, endless cycle of grace.

I am nearing the wonder of Communion.

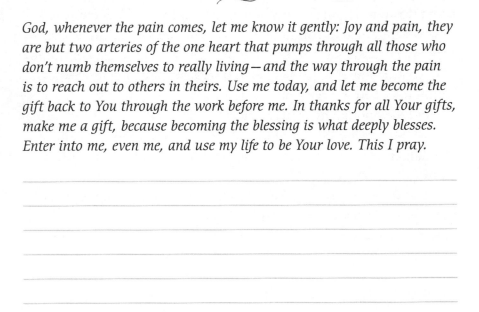

God, whenever the pain comes, let me know it gently: Joy and pain, they are but two arteries of the one heart that pumps through all those who don't numb themselves to really living—and the way through the pain is to reach out to others in theirs. Use me today, and let me become the gift back to You through the work before me. In thanks for all Your gifts, make me a gift, because becoming the blessing is what deeply blesses. Enter into me, even me, and use my life to be Your love. This I pray.

count 1,000 ways
He loves you . . .

1. _____
2. _____
3. _____
4. _____
5. _____
6. _____
7. _____
8. _____
9. _____
10. _____
11. _____
12. _____
13. _____
14. _____
15. _____
16. _____
17. _____
18. _____
19. _____
20. _____
21. _____
22. _____
23. _____
24. _____
25. _____
26. _____

Give thanks in all circumstances; for this is God's will for you in Christ Jesus.
—1 Thessalonians 5:18

27. _____
28. _____
29. _____
30. _____
31. _____
32. _____
33. _____
34. _____
35. _____
36. _____
37. _____
38. _____
39. _____
40. _____
41. _____
42. _____
43. _____
44. _____
45. _____
46. _____
47. _____
48. _____
49. _____
50. _____

51. _____
52. _____
53. _____
54. _____
55. _____
56. _____
57. _____
58. _____
59. _____
60. _____
61. _____
62. _____
63. _____
64. _____
65. _____
66. _____
67. _____
68. _____
69. _____
70. _____
71. _____
72. _____
73. _____
74. _____
75. _____
76. _____

When I only give thanks for some things,
aren't I likely to miss giving God glory in most things?

77. _____
78. _____
79. _____
80. _____
81. _____
82. _____
83. _____
84. _____
85. _____
86. _____
87. _____
88. _____
89. _____
90. _____
91. _____
92. _____
93. _____
94. _____
95. _____
96. _____
97. _____
98. _____
99. _____
100. _____

101. _____

102. _____

103. _____

104. _____

105. _____

106. _____

107. _____

108. _____

109. _____

110. _____

111. _____

112. _____

113. _____

114. _____

115. _____

116. _____

117. _____

118. _____

119. _____

120. _____

121. _____

122. _____

123. _____

124. _____

125. _____

126. _____

To thank God in all is to bend the knee in allegiance to God,
who alone knows all.

127. _____
128. _____
129. _____
130. _____
131. _____
132. _____
133. _____
134. _____
135. _____
136. _____
137. _____
138. _____
139. _____
140. _____
141. _____
142. _____
143. _____
144. _____
145. _____
146. _____
147. _____
148. _____
149. _____
150. _____

151. _____
152. _____
153. _____
154. _____
155. _____
156. _____
157. _____
158. _____
159. _____
160. _____
161. _____
162. _____
163. _____
164. _____
165. _____
166. _____
167. _____
168. _____
169. _____
170. _____
171. _____
172. _____
173. _____
174. _____
175. _____
176. _____

If you want to change the world, pick up your pen.
—Martin Luther

177. _____
178. _____
179. _____
180. _____
181. _____
182. _____
183. _____
184. _____
185. _____
186. _____
187. _____
188. _____
189. _____
190. _____
191. _____
192. _____
193. _____
194. _____
195. _____
196. _____
197. _____
198. _____
199. _____
200. _____

201.

202.

203.

204.

205.

206.

207.

208.

209.

210.

211.

212.

213.

214.

215.

216.

217.

218.

219.

220.

221.

222.

223.

224.

225.

226.

Our thanks to God is our witness to the goodness of God
when Satan and all world would sneer at us to recant.

227. _____

228. _____

229. _____

230. _____

231. _____

232. _____

233. _____

234. _____

235. _____

236. _____

237. _____

238. _____

239. _____

240. _____

241. _____

242. _____

243. _____

244. _____

245. _____

246. _____

247. _____

248. _____

249. _____

250. _____

251. _____

252. _____

253. _____

254. _____

255. _____

256. _____

257. _____

258. _____

259. _____

260. _____

261. _____

262. _____

263. _____

264. _____

265. _____

266. _____

267. _____

268. _____

269. _____

270. _____

271. _____

272. _____

273. _____

274. _____

275. _____

276. _____

Our perennial spiritual and psychological task is to look at things familiar until they become unfamiliar again.

—G. K. Chesterton

277. _____

278. _____

279. _____

280. _____

281. _____

282. _____

283. _____

284. _____

285. _____

286. _____

287. _____

288. _____

289. _____

290. _____

291. _____

292. _____

293. _____

294. _____

295. _____

296. _____

297. _____

298. _____

299. _____

300. _____

301. _____

302. _____

303. _____

304. _____

305. _____

306. _____

307. _____

308. _____

309. _____

310. _____

311. _____

312. _____

313. _____

314. _____

315. _____

316. _____

317: _____

318. _____

319. _____

320. _____

321. _____

322. _____

323. _____

324. _____

325. _____

326. _____

That which I refuse to thank Christ for,
I refuse to believe Christ can redeem.

327. _____
328. _____
329. _____
330. _____
331. _____
332. _____
333. _____
334. _____
335. _____
336. _____
337. _____
338. _____
339. _____
340. _____
341. _____
342. _____
343. _____
344. _____
345. _____
346. _____
347. _____
348. _____
349. _____
350. _____

351. _____

352. _____

353. _____

354. _____

355. _____

356. _____

357. _____

358. _____

359. _____

360. _____

361. _____

362. _____

363. _____

364. _____

365. _____

366. _____

367. _____

368. _____

369. _____

370. _____

371. _____

372. _____

373. _____

374. _____

375. _____

376. _____

Giving thanks in hard times makes the canyon of pain into a megaphone to proclaim the ultimate goodness of God.

377. _____
378. _____
379. _____
380. _____
381. _____
382. _____
383. _____
384. _____
385. _____
386. _____
387. _____
388. _____
389. _____
390. _____
391. _____
392. _____
393. _____
394. _____
395. _____
396. _____
397. _____
398. _____
399. _____
400. _____

401. _____
402. _____
403. _____
404. _____
405. _____
406. _____
407. _____
408. _____
409. _____
410. _____
411. _____
412. _____
413. _____
414. _____
415. _____
416. _____
417. _____
418. _____
419. _____
420. _____
421. _____
422. _____
423. _____
424. _____
425. _____
426. _____

It is in the process of being worshiped that God communicates His presence to men.
—C. S. Lewis

427. _____

428. _____

429. _____

430. _____

431. _____

432. _____

433. _____

434. _____

435. _____

436. _____

437. _____

438. _____

439. _____

440. _____

441. _____

442. _____

443. _____

444. _____

445. _____

446. _____

447. _____

448. _____

449. _____

450. _____

451. _____

452. _____

453. _____

454. _____

455. _____

456. _____

457. _____

458. _____

459. _____

460. _____

461. _____

462. _____

463. _____

464. _____

465. _____

466. _____

467. _____

468. _____

469. _____

470. _____

471. _____

472. _____

473. _____

474. _____

475. _____

476. _____

It is suffering that has the realest possibility
to bear down and deliver grace.

477. _____

478. _____

479. _____

480. _____

481. _____

482. _____

483. _____

484. _____

485. _____

486. _____

487. _____

488. _____

489. _____

490. _____

491. _____

492. _____

493. _____

494. _____

495. _____

496. _____

497. _____

498. _____

499. _____

500. _____

501. _____
502. _____
503. _____
504. _____
505. _____
506. _____
507. _____
508. _____
509. _____
510. _____
511. _____
512. _____
513. _____
514. _____
515. _____
516. _____
517. _____
518. _____
519. _____
520. _____
521. _____
522. _____
523. _____
524. _____
525. _____
526. _____

No gift unrecognized as coming from God is at its own best ...
when in all gifts we find Him, then in Him we shall find all things.
—George MacDonald

527. _____
528. _____
529. _____
530. _____
531. _____
532. _____
533. _____
534. _____
535. _____
536. _____
537. _____
538. _____
539. _____
540. _____
541. _____
542. _____
543. _____
544. _____
545. _____
546. _____
547. _____
548. _____
549. _____
550. _____

551.

552.

553.

554.

555.

556.

557.

558.

559.

560.

561.

562.

563.

564.

565.

566.

567.

568.

569.

570.

571.

572.

573.

574.

575.

576.

I only deepen the wound of a hurting world
when I neglect to give thanks.

577. _____

578. _____

579. _____

580. _____

581. _____

582. _____

583. _____

584. _____

585. _____

586. _____

587. _____

588. _____

589. _____

590. _____

591. _____

592. _____

593. _____

594. _____

595. _____

596. _____

597. _____

598. _____

599. _____

600. _____

601. _____

602. _____

603. _____

604. _____

605. _____

606. _____

607. _____

608. _____

609. _____

610. _____

611. _____

612. _____

613. _____

614. _____

615. _____

616. _____

617. _____

618. _____

619. _____

620. _____

621. _____

622. _____

623. _____

624. _____

625. _____

626. _____

*Who feels such gratitude for their salvation in Christ
that they feel such affection for Christ?*

627. _____

628. _____

629. _____

630. _____

631. _____

632. _____

633. _____

634. _____

635. _____

636. _____

637. _____

638. _____

639. _____

640. _____

641. _____

642. _____

643. _____

644. _____

645. _____

646. _____

647. _____

648. _____

649. _____

650. _____

651. _____
652. _____
653. _____
654. _____
655. _____
656. _____
657. _____
658. _____
659. _____
660. _____
661. _____
662. _____
663. _____
664. _____
665. _____
666. _____
667. _____
668. _____
669. _____
670. _____
671. _____
672. _____
673. _____
674. _____
675. _____
676. _____

Out of his fullness we have all received grace in place of grace already given.
—John 1:16

677. _____
678. _____
679. _____
680. _____
681. _____
682. _____
683. _____
684. _____
685. _____
686. _____
687. _____
688. _____
689. _____
690. _____
691. _____
692. _____
693. _____
694. _____
695. _____
696. _____
697. _____
698. _____
699. _____
700. _____

701. _____

702. _____

703. _____

704. _____

705. _____

706. _____

707. _____

708. _____

709. _____

710. _____

711. _____

712. _____

713. _____

714. _____

715. _____

716. _____

717. _____

718. _____

719. _____

720. _____

721. _____

722. _____

723. _____

724. _____

725. _____

726. _____

Our fall is always first a failure to give thanks.

727. _____

728. _____

729. _____

730. _____

731. _____

732. _____

733. _____

734. _____

735. _____

736. _____

737. _____

738. _____

739. _____

740. _____

741. _____

742. _____

743. _____

744. _____

745. _____

746. _____

747. _____

748. _____

749. _____

750. _____

751. _____
752. _____
753. _____
754. _____
755. _____
756. _____
757. _____
758. _____
759. _____
760. _____
761. _____
762. _____
763. _____
764. _____
765. _____
766. _____
767. _____
768. _____
769. _____
770. _____
771. _____
772. _____
773. _____
774. _____
775. _____
776. _____

Gratitude bestows reverence, allowing us to encounter everyday epiphanies, those transcendent moments of awe that change forever how we experience life and the world. —Sarah Ban Breathnach

777. _____
778. _____
779. _____
780. _____
781. _____
782. _____
783. _____
784. _____
785. _____
786. _____
787. _____
788. _____
789. _____
790. _____
791. _____
792. _____
793. _____
794. _____
795. _____
796. _____
797. _____
798. _____
799. _____
800. _____

801. _____

802. _____

803. _____

804. _____

805. _____

806. _____

807. _____

808. _____

809. _____

810. _____

811. _____

812. _____

813. _____

814. _____

815. _____

816. _____

817. _____

818. _____

819. _____

820. _____

821. _____

822. _____

823. _____

824. _____

825. _____

826. _____

In a broken world—when we remember how He blesses, loves us,
when we recollect His goodnesses to us, we heal—we re-member.

827. _____

828. _____

829. _____

830. _____

831. _____

832. _____

833. _____

834. _____

835. _____

836. _____

837. _____

838. _____

839. _____

840. _____

841. _____

842. _____

843. _____

844. _____

845. _____

846. _____

847. _____

848. _____

849. _____

850. _____

851. _____

852. _____

853. _____

854. _____

855. _____

856. _____

857. _____

858. _____

859. _____

860. _____

861. _____

862. _____

863. _____

864. _____

865. _____

866. _____

867. _____

868. _____

869. _____

870. _____

871. _____

872. _____

873. _____

874. _____

875. _____

876. _____

The unthankful heart ... discovers no mercies; but let the thankful heart sweep through the day and, as the magnet finds the iron, so it will find, in every hour, some heavenly blessings. —Henry Ward Beecher

877. _____
878. _____
879. _____
880. _____
881. _____
882. _____
883. _____
884. _____
885. _____
886. _____
887. _____
888. _____
889. _____
890. _____
891. _____
892. _____
893. _____
694. _____
895. _____
896. _____
897. _____
898. _____
899. _____
900. _____

901. _____

902. _____

903. _____

904. _____

905. _____

906. _____

907. _____

908. _____

909. _____

910. _____

911. _____

912. _____

913. _____

914. _____

915. _____

916. _____

917. _____

918. _____

919. _____

920. _____

921. _____

922. _____

923. _____

924. _____

925. _____

926. _____

I accept this is the way to begin, and all hard things come in due time and with practice. Yet now wisps of cheese tell me gentle that this is the first secret step into eucharisteo's miracle.

927. _____

928. _____

929. _____

930. _____

931. _____

932. _____

933. _____

934. _____

935. _____

936. _____

937. _____

938. _____

939. _____

940. _____

941. _____

942. _____

943. _____

944. _____

945. _____

946. _____

947. _____

948. _____

949. _____

950. _____

951. _____

952. _____

953. _____

954. _____

955. _____

956. _____

957. _____

958. _____

959. _____

960. _____

961. _____

962. _____

963. _____

964. _____

965. _____

966. _____

967. _____

968. _____

969. _____

970. _____

971. _____

972. _____

973. _____

974. _____

975. _____

976. _____

See what great love the Father has lavished on us,
that we should be called children of God!
—1 John 3:1

977. _____

978. _____

979. _____

980. _____

981. _____

982. _____

983. _____

984. _____

985. _____

986. _____

987. _____

988. _____

989. _____

990. _____

991. _____

992. _____

993. _____

994. _____

995. _____

996. _____

997. _____

998. _____

999. _____

1000. _____

acknowledgments

Thanks be to God.

For Bill, who has stood beside me on his knees, and Mick the visionary, who chiseled relentlessly because he saw His grace in stones, and Tonia, who is an unwavering Jonathan. Your fellowship is a gift.

For Dirk, who has gently pastored every word, every encounter, like his Shepherd; for Sandy, who has marched the walls in faithful prayer, tender wisdom, and blessed friendship; for Tom and Don and Tracy and Jennifer, the dream team that has championed for His glory!

For every reader at www.aholyexperience.com — that we can do life together? That you'd take me anyway? It is one of the most humbling privileges imaginable, to do community with you. Reaching over right now and squeezing your hand and whispering, "God knows your name and your story and He cups you close and He is always good and you are always loved and may you know it right now, in your marrow and your bone, the wooing love of Christ."

For my mama, who has served and loved and given like Jesus — He's multiplied all you've offered Him and the beauty of your gift takes away my breath. Thank you, Mama — a thousand times over, thank you. For Molly, who has served and supported and is my Barnabas sister. You and Mama have been Aaron and Hur.

For Caleb and Joshua, Hope and Levi, Malakai and Shalom. Thank you for always saying, "Please — read just one more page?" But mostly, for making your lives into this story that's taken my breath away. You all have been my favorite chapters.

For Darryl, whose life whispers to all the timid, *Fly. He means for us to fly on wings of grace.* There is only one you.

For Father, Son, and Holy Spirit. We have received nothing unless it is given to us from heaven (John 3:27). For all this grace upon grace upon grace — we can only murmur:

Thanks be to God.

notes

1. Mark Buchanan, *The Holy Wild* (Colorado Springs: Multnomah, 2005), 105.

2. Ibid., 106.

3. Ibid., 108.

4. Robert Frost, "A Winter Eden," www.portitude.org/literature/frost/pt-winter_
eden.php (accessed July 10, 2012).

5. Gilbert Keith Chesterton, *A Short History of England* (Teddington, Middlesex, UK:
Echo Library, 2008), 30.

6. Augustine, *Confessions of Saint Augustine*, book 10, chapter 21.

7. Quoted in Belden Lane, *Ravished by Beauty: The Surprising Legacy of Reformed
Spirituality* (New York: Oxford University Press, 2011), 65.

8. Ibid., 66.

9. Ibid.

10. Ibid., 69.

11. Ibid., 82.

12. Mark Buchanan, *The Rest of God: Restoring Your Soul by Restoring Your Sabbath*
(Nashville: Nelson, 2007), 45, emphasis added.

13. John Piper, *When I Don't Desire God: How to Fight for Joy* (Wheaton, Ill.: Crossway,
2004), 124.

14. Desiderius Erasmus, "*Diluculum,* or The Early Rising," in *The Colloquies of Erasmus*
(London: Reeves and Turner, 1878), 2:212.

15. C. S. Lewis, *God in the Dock* (Grand Rapids: Eerdmans, 1994), 52.

16. "New Letters of R. L. Stevenson," in *Harper's Monthly Magazine*, vol. 104, eds.
Henry Mills Alden, Thomas Bucklin Wells, and Lee Foster Hartman (New York:
Harper, 1902), 126.

17. John Piper, "From His Fullness We Have All Received, Grace Upon Grace,"
www.desiringgod.org/ResourceLibrary/Sermons/ByDate/2008/3394_From_His_
Fullness_We_Have_All_Received_Grace_Upon_Grace/ (accessed July 10, 2012).

18. C. S. Lewis, *The Great Divorce* (New York: Macmillan, 1946), 77.

19. A. W. Tozer, *The Pursuit of God* (Camp Hill, Pa.: Christian Publications, 1982), 73.

20. C. S. Lewis, "The Weight of Glory," in *The Weight of Glory and Other Addresses* (Grand Rapids: Eerdmans, 1965), 12–13.

21. Teresa of Avila, quoted in Amy Welborn, *The Loyola Kids Book of Saints* (Chicago: Loyola, 2001), 87.

22. G. K. Chesterton, *Orthodoxy* (Rockville, Md.: Serenity, 2009), 19.

23. Quoted in G. B. F. Hallock, "The Cultivation of Humility," *Herald and Presbyter* 90 (December 24, 1919): 8.

24. Timothy Keller, "The Advent of Humility," *Christianity Today*, December 22, 2008, www.christianitytoday.com/ct/2008/december/20.51.html (accessed July 10, 2012).

25. Dennis Linn, Sheila Fabricant Linn, and Matthew Linn, *Sleeping with Bread: Holding What Gives You Life* (Mahwah N.J.: Paulist, 1995), 1.

26. Lewis, "The Weight of Glory," 10.

27. Dennis Lennon, *Fuelling the Fire: Fresh Thinking on Prayer* (Queensway, UK: Scripture Union, 2005), 43, emphasis added.

28. Chesterton, *Orthodoxy*, 55.

29. Quoted in Wilhelm Odelberg, *Les Prix Nobel 1986* (Stockholm: Nobel Foundation, 1987).

30. Charles H. Spurgeon, "The Simplicity and Sublimity of Salvation," http://articles.ochristian.com/article8386.shtml (accessed July 10, 2012).

31. J. R. Miller, "The Thanksgiving Lesson," www.gracegems.org/Miller/thanksgiving_lesson.htm (accessed July 12, 2012).

32. Peter Kreeft, "Joy," www.peterkreeft.com/topics/joy.htm (accessed July 12, 2012), emphasis added.

33. Jean-Pierre de Caussade, quoted in *A Guide to Prayer for All God's People*, Rueben Job and Norman Shawchuck, eds. (Nashville: Upper Room, 1990), 244.

34. Annie Dillard, *Pilgrim at Tinker Creek* (New York: HarperPerennial, 1998), 33.

35. Dorothy Sayers, *Letters to a Diminished Church* (Nashville: Nelson, 2004), 143.

36. Chesterton, *Orthodoxy*, 138.

37. Will Bowen, *A Complaint-Free World* (New York: Doubleday, 2007), 116, 118.

38. Ibid., 121.

39. Ibid.

Ann Voskamp is a farmer's wife, the home-educating mama to a half-dozen exuberant kids, and the author of the *New York Times* bestseller *One Thousand Gifts: A Dare to Live Fully Right Where You Are.* She tells stories. She takes pictures. She sees the whole earth full of the glory of God. A columnist with DaySpring, a contributing editor to Laity Lodge's The High Calling, and a writer of articles featured in *WORLD* magazine, *The Huffington Post*, and *Christianity Today*, Ann partners with Compassion International as a global advocate for needy children. The poor have made her rich, and telling the stories of those who need a voice has changed her own story. Ann can be found writing about messy grace and a magnificent God at her daily online journal: www.aholyexperience.com. Visit Ann's website at: www.onethousandgifts.com.

Write to Zondervan authors or their estates in care of Zondervan. Your mail will be forwarded as soon as possible, but please note that the author might not be able to respond personally. Email zauthor@zondervan.com or send postal mail to:

Ann Voskamp
c/o Zondervan
ATTN: Author Care
5300 Patterson SE
Grand Rapids, MI 49530

One Thousand Gifts

A Dare to Live Fully
Right Where You Are

Ann Voskamp

Just like you, Ann Voskamp hungers to live her one life well. Forget the bucket lists that have us escaping our everyday lives for exotic experiences. "How," Ann wondered, "do we find joy in the midst of deadlines, debt, drama, and daily duties? What does the Christ-life really look like when your days are gritty, long—and sometimes even dark? How is God even here?"

In *One Thousand Gifts*, Ann invites you to embrace everyday blessings and embark on the transformative spiritual discipline of chronicling God's gifts. It's only in this expressing of gratitude for the life we already have that we discover the life we've always wanted … a life we can take, give thanks for, and break for others. We come to feel and know the impossible right down in our bones: we are wildly loved—by God. Let Ann's beautiful, heart-aching stories of the everyday give you a way of seeing that opens your eyes to ordinary amazing grace, a way of being present to God that makes you deeply happy, and a way of living that is finally fully alive.

Come live the best dare of all!

Selections from One Thousand Gifts

Finding Joy in What Really Matters

Ann Voskamp,
New York Times *bestselling author*

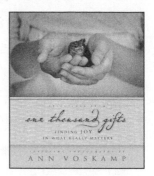

What if joy were possible—right where you are? Inspiring hundreds of thousands of readers to wake to their own wondrous lives, the *New York Times* bestseller *One Thousand Gifts: A Dare to Live Fully Right Where You Are* shares the journey of one woman facing her own hard, dark days and hidden fears, and stumbling straight into the answer of life's great riddle: How do you discover joy—right here and now?

Selections from One Thousand Gifts features powerful, life-changing passages from Voskamp's compelling story and her own exquisite photography, framing a seemingly ordinary, gritty life around true amazing grace. Because if joy is a matter of gratitude, and gratitude is a matter of perspective, then giving thanks changes not only your perspective but also your life.

Open these lyrical pages and slow down to discover the joy you've always been looking for.

Come find God in the moments!

Available in stores and online!

one thousand gifts

FREE APP
iPhone • iPad

ONE THOUSAND GIFTS, A THOUSAND THANKS

How do you find every day, amazing grace in the midst of deadlines, debt, drama, and daily duties?

New York Times bestselling author Ann Voskamp offers this practical, radical answer: by giving thanks for the life you already have, to find the life you've always wanted.

This exclusive mobile app will help you do just that. Capture your gifts. Count your blessings. Share your joy as it happens on the way to your own one thousand gifts.

SHARE YOUR GIFTS WHEREVER YOU ARE

The simple moments in life that bring true happiness — a high pile of freshly grated cheese, the music of your child's carefree giggles — too often pass us by without a second thought. The *One Thousand Gifts* mobile app will help you slow down and catch God in the moment.

THE ONE THOUSAND GIFTS MOBILE APP FEATURES:

- Quotes on awakening to the joy-filled power of grace and gratitude ... to help get you started
- Photos and texts of your gifts ... to keep you going
- A one-tap option to instantly share your captured gifts on Facebook, Twitter, and Flickr ... to keep your friends and your family inspired on their way to their one thousand gifts